The Philosophy of Malebranche

THE PHILOSOPHY OF
MALEBRANCHE

BY

WILLIAM CURTIS SWABEY, A. M.

A THESIS

Presented to the Faculty of the Graduate School
of Cornell University for the Degree of
Doctor of Philosophy

1921

PREFACE

In the following pages, I have attempted merely
to give an accurate historical account of the main
philosophical opinions of Father Malebranche; the
perhaps more important task of making a critical ap-
praisal of the truth of these opinions has been largely
left to some future date. It is, at any rate, clear that
the system of Malebranche, as a chapter in the history
of the Platonic tradition, deserves more consideration
than it has hitherto received. I must take this occasion to express my gratitude to my teachers at Cornell
University, and especially to Professor J. E. Creigh-
ton, without whose kindly encouragement this disser-
tation would never have been completed.

THE AUTHOR.

S

478424

TABLE OF CONTENTS

THE PHILOSOPHY OF MALEBRANCHE.

CHAPTER I: INTRODUCTION.

Bouillier, in his splendid *Histoire de la philosophie cartési-* ✓
enne, declares that Malebranche is the greatest metaphysician
of France after Descartes.[1] Few would contest this statement.[2]
Now Malebranche was a member of the Congregation of the
Oratory of Jesus. This latter may be described as an associa-
tion of priests, devoted to prayer, study and teaching.[3] Its members were not monks, and it had neither secret constitution nor
solemn vows, other than those of the priesthood itself.[3] They
were simply priests united by a common love of piety and science, living in common according to the ideals of the primitive
church. Upon entering the Oratory, a priest did not renounce
his liberty, but was always as free to leave as he had been to
enter; and each of the members preserved a certain independence, being permitted to devote himself to the study for which
he felt most inclination.[4] The Oratory was distinguished by a
happy combination of philosophy, science, scholarship and theology.[4] Its liberal spirit is seen in the rule which dispensed a
member who showed some special aptitude for study from all
other duties.[4]

The famous ecclesiastic, Bossuet, declared, in his *Oraison
Funèbre du P Bourgoing,* speaking of Cardinal de Bérulle, that
his "great love for the Church inspired him to form a company
to which he desired to give no other spirit than that of the
Church, nor other rules than the canons, nor other superiors
than the bishops, nor other bonds than charity, nor other solemn
oaths than those of baptism and priesthood, a company where a
holy liberty creates a holy obligation, where there is obedience
without dependence and government without command, where
all authority is in gentleness and where respect is not aided by
fear; a company in which a charity that banishes fear works a
great miracle and in which with no yoke charity is able, not only
to captivate, but also to annihilate self-will; a company in which
to form true priests they are lead to the source of truth, where

---

[1] Bouillier, *op cit*, Ed of 1854, Vol II, p 32 Henceforth referred to as Bouillier simply Unless otherwise stated, the references are all to Vol II

[2] J. Simon, in his able Introduction to his edition to the *Oeuvres de Malebranche*
(XLIII), says· *"Ce fou de Malebranche est une de nos grandes gloires nationales, ses
visions métaphysiques sont une école de sagesse et de profonde philosophie, et plaise
à Dieu pour l'honneur de la philosophie et le progrès de l'esprit humain, qu'il nous
puisse naître des rêveurs comme lui!"*

[3] Bouillier, p 4

[4] Bouillier, p 5

they have always at hand the holy books to seek in them without rest the letter by the mind, the spirit by prayer, depth by retreat, etc.''[5]

As Bouillier remarks, Bossuet's praise marks the difference between the Jesuits and the Oratory.[5] And just as these two societies were opposed in spirit, so they were opposed in philosophy. Cardinal de Bérulle gave the Oratory its initial tendency.[6] His admiration was, in the first place, for St. Augustine, a fact which made the Oratory always open to suspicion of Jansenism.[6] And, through St. Augustine, the Oratory came to esteem Plato more than Aristotle even before the time of Descartes.[6] Thus certain of the early Fathers of the Congregation sought to introduce the Platonic doctrine. Father Fournenc was the author of a complete course of philosophy which appeared in 1665 in which he declared his intention of uniting the spirit of Plato with the true philosophy of Aristotle.[6] But when the Cartesian philosophy came into vogue the original Platonic tendency of the Oratory was at first forgotten.[7]

However much influence de Bérulle may have exerted to the advantage of Plato, his friendship and admiration for Descartes were even more influential in determining the philosophical tendency of the Oratory. As Baillet tells us in his *Vie de Descartes* the discourse of Descartes on a certain occasion so impressed the Cardinal that the latter sought private conference with him, and gave him great encouragement in his project of philosophical reform.[7] However, it was not de Bérulle who actually introduced the study of Descartes into the Oratory so much as Fathers Gibieuf and La Barde, who were zealous partisans of Descartes.[7] And the friendship of the Oratory was undoubtedly one of the causes of the success of Descartes' philosophy.

Now Malebranche was not without predecessors in the Oratory in uniting the spirit of Descartes with that of Augustine and Plato; nevertheless his philosophy was the most brilliant and successful performance of this feat. Father André Martin, who is known under the pseudonym of Ambrosius Victor, seems to have been his immediate precursor and master[8] André Martin was a professor of philosophy at the *college d'Angers* and was one of the first to introduce the doctrine of Descartes into philosophical teaching.[9] This latter proceeding aroused the authorities of the college to the extent that he was ordered to confine his teaching to the doctrine of Aristotle.[9] Later in his life he was suspected of Jansenism and for that reason suspended from the chair of philosophy at Saumur.[10] In his *Philosophia Chris-*

---

[5] Bouillier, p. 6
[6] Bouillier, p 7
[7] Bouillier, p. 8
[8] Bouillier, p 10
[9] Bouillier, p 10
[10] Bouillier, p 11

tiana, published under the name of Ambrosius Victor, he develops his views at length, claiming the authority of Augustine; this work is the most noteworthy predecessor of the *Recherche de la vérité*.[10] In this *Philosophia Christiana*, André Martin expounds the doctrine of St. Augustine concerning God, man, animals, and concerning many other topics, but it is not difficult to see that it is always Descartes who is speaking through Augustine.[10] Thus in his *Sanctus Augustinus de anima bestiarum* he claims to find many arguments in Augustine that support the Cartesian theory of animal automatism.[10] But André Martin is above all the precursor of Malebranche in the way in which he emphasizes Augustine's version of Platonism in regard to the eternal truths and the divine ideas.[10] He held that there were, in the divine mind, ideas of all creatures, just as in the mind of an artist there is an idea of his work; and that God does not draw his knowledge of his creatures from his creatures themselves but from his own ideas of them.[11] We say that we behold creatures, but in truth we behold their ideas in God, although their ideas have neither extension nor figure.[11] And, lastly, among the Oratorians before the time of Malebranche who were followers of Descartes, we have the learned Father Poisson, who was a commentator on the *Discourse on Method* and the geometry of Descartes.[12] Thus the Oratory was always characterized by an idealistic tendency and preferred Plato to Aristotle, St. Augustine to St. Thomas.[12] Descartes was only received by the Oratory with an intermixture of elements borrowed from Plato and Augustine, for, even before Malebranche, the Oratory inclined to the doctrine of a divine reason enlightening men, *i. e.*, to the notion of vision in God, and to the tendency to justify faith by reason.[12]

The contrast between the Oratory and the Society of Jesus is very striking, and may be compared to the medieval conflict between Franciscans and Dominicans.[13] The Oratory represents the spirit of rationalism or idealism; the Jesuits that of empiricism. The first society favored Plato and Descartes; the second, Aristotle and Gassendi.[13] Indeed, as Bouillier says, the historic mission of the Congregation of the Oratory seems to have been to have defended throughout the seventeenth and eighteenth centuries the principles of Platonic idealism.[13]

Now, Nicolas Malebranche was born in Paris in 1638, of a Nicolas Malebranche, a secretary to the king, and of Catherine de Lauzon, whose brother was vice-regent of Canada.[14] He was the last of ten children, according to Adry, and of thirteen, ac-

[10] Bouillier, p 11
[11] Bouillier, p 12
[13] Bouillier, p 13
[13] Bouillier, p 14
[14] In regard to Malebranche's life, I am following the later account given in Joly, *Malebranche*, Paris, 1901, henceforth referred to as Joly. See Joly p 1.

cording to André. His constitution and physical frame were
very defective; he suffered from curvature of the spine and a
very narrow chest.[15] From an early age, according to André,
he felt a desire to withdraw from the world.[15] At sixteen years
he followed the course of the *college de la Marche.*[16] There he
studied under a certain M. Rouillard, a peripatetic, who, however, succeeded only in disgusting him with the scholastic system.[16] He hoped for more satisfaction in the theology of the
Sorbonne, which he studied for three years. But he found this
study equally unsatisfactory.[17] Feeling a profound need of re-
tirement, and having lost his mother and his father, the one
shortly after the other, he took, in 1660, steps to enter the Congregation of the Oratory.[18] At first he applied himself to works
of erudition and historical criticism, but without success.[19] Up
to the age of twenty-six, in spite of a rather vivid interest in St.
Augustine,[20] he could not be said to have found his philosophical vocation.[21] One day he happened upon Descartes' post-
humous and incomplete *Treatise on Man* in which Descartes endeavors to give a mechanistic account of the human constitution;
he was so fascinated with the clarity and connection of ideas
that, as he said, he was frequently obliged to interrupt his
reading by reason of the violent palpitations of his heart.[22]

Malebranche thus became a philosopher and a Cartesian at
the same time; he now abandoned Greek, Hebrew, and history,
and for ten years buried himself in the philosophy of Descartes,
which he was interested in reconciling with that of Augustine.[22]
He then produced the first volume of his *Recherche de la vérité*
(1675), covering Sense, Imagination, and Understanding.[23] In
the course of the next year (1676), he published the second volume, covering the Natural Inclinations, the Passions, and Method.[23] The *Recherche de la vérité* was highly successful and the
Oratory voted its author thanks and congratulations.[24]

In 1677 he published his *Conversationes métaphysiques et
chrétiennes.*[25] In 1680 appeared his *Traité de la nature et de
la grace,* which is his most important work from a specifically
theological standpoint.[25] This work was the occasion of his great
quarrel with Arnauld.[25] In 1684, he published his *Traité de
morale,* which we shall review in this study. In 1684, we have

[15] *Cf* André, *La vie de Malebranche avec l'histoire de ses ouvrages, Bibliotheque
Oratorienne,* 1886 Joly, p 2
[16] Joly, p 2
[17] *Cf* André, *op cit* , p 6
[18] Joly, p 4.
[19] Bouillier, p 15
[20] Joly, p 14
[21] Bouillier, p 15
[22] Bouillier, p 15, and Joly, p 14
[23] Bouillier p 16   A Latin translation of the Sixth Book of the *Recherche* was
put on the Index along with certain other of Malebranche's works, see Joly, p 40
[24] Bouillier, p 16, and Joly, p 23f
[25] Joly, p 27f   It was condemned at Rome in 1690. Bouillier, p 17

his *Méditations métaphysiques et chrétiennes,* which, although relatively important, is yet not of any crucial significance. In 1688, we have the *Entretiens sur la métaphysique et sur la religion*[26] This work, which we take as the basis of our account of Malebranche's metaphysics, as Bouillier says, "*contient toute la doctrine de Malebranche dans son plus haute et son dernier développement.*"[26] In 1697, we have the *Traité de l'amour de Dieu,* in 1708, the *Entretiens d'un philosophe chinois sur l'existence et la nature de Dieu,* and in 1715, the very year of his death, we have *Réflexions sur la prémotion physique.*[27]

These various writings brought him in the course of his life into many controversies, all of which were distasteful to him, for his genius was more dogmatic and constructive than polemical in character.[28] His love of repose was his dominant passion, but he was forced to spend the greater part of his life in controversies of various sorts. Of these struggles, the longest and keenest was with the great Jansenist and Port Royal leader, Antoine Arnauld.[29] In this controversy, as Victor Cousin pointed out, Malebranche has the timidity and obstinacy of the recluse.[30] He repeats his arguments without variation rather than analyzes the thoughts of his opponent.[30] His greatness lay in constructive thinking rather than in dialectic.

Malebranche's literary style was one great cause of his success, Fontenelle, Bayle, André, Daguesseau, Arnauld, Bossuet, Diderot and Voltaire are mentioned by Bouillier as having specifically praised the style of Malebranche.[31] The same author remarks that Malebranche joins to the "perfume of spirituality," or "mystical grace," the vivid and sharp style of Pascal and La Bruyere.[32] In fact, the beauty of his style does consist in his way of combining the abstract and the concrete, in his happy faculty of giving a kind of substantial existence to the objects of the most abstruse thought.

Malebranche was, like Descartes, at the same time, metaphysician, mathematician and physicist.[32] ⁓He throughout, like Plato himself, rests his thought upon mathematical examples.⁓ He was a friend of the Marquise de l'Hopital, the famous mathematician, and explained the latter's analysis of the infinitely small to the young Mairan, who later carried on with him a very important philosophical correspondence.[32] He had a controversy with Leibniz on the laws of motion and with very honorable good faith modified his views in the last edition of the *Recherche*

[26] Bouillier, p 17   Joly, p 37f
[27] Bouillier, p 17   It is greatly to be desired that the proposal, which D Roustan so ably defends (*Pour une édition de Malebranche, Revue de metaphysique et de morale,* Vol XXIII, p 163) be realized!
[28] Bouillier, p 17
[29] Joly, p 77f
[30] Bouillier, p 18
[31] Bouillier, p 19
[32] Bouillier, p 21

de la vérité.[32] In the field of physics he modified Descartes' theory of the vortices.[32] In 1699, he was made an honorary member of the Academy of Science, and in the Academy had a long controversy with Regis, whom the student of Descartes will remember, on the subject of the apparent size of the moon on the horizon, which terminated to his advantage in a statement signed by the most prominent mathematicians of the Academy.[33] But he did not esteem as highly the empirical sciences, such as chemistry or astronomy, as he did mathematics and mathematical physics.[33] As he says in the Preface to the *Recherche de la vérité*: "Men are not born to become astronomers or chemists, and to pass their lives attached to a telescope or a furnace and then draw useless conclusions from their laborious observations."[34] He had still less admiration for historical science, for erudition, for the study and criticism of language.[35] On the other hand, he had a very vivid interest in insects.[35]

For Malebranche, all philosophy before the time of Descartes was barbarism, while for Descartes Malebranche had only profound admiration and veneration.[36] He says in the *Recherche*[37]: "Those who read the works of this learned man feel a secret joy in being born in a century and in a country fortunate enough to spare us the trouble of seeking in past centuries, among pagans, at the extremities of the earth, among barbarians and foreigners, a teacher to instruct us in the truth." But, as Bouillier says, Malebranche makes only slight mention of Plato. while he often cites Aristotle, whom he regarded as the "prince of false philosophers."[38] He had no higher opinion of the great philosophers of the School, with the exception of Augustine, who, indeed, is hardly to be considered a scholastic.[39]

Malebranche passed the greater part of his life in Paris in a cell of the Saint-Honoré Oratory, absorbed in meditation, as we may say, upon divine things.[39] He pleasantly refers to himself in the *Entretiens sur la métaphysique* as a *méditatif*, as a *taciturne méditatif*.[40] In spite of his withdrawal from the life

---

[33] Bouillier, p. 22

[34] *Op. cit.*, p. XV

[35] Bouillier, p 23   *Cf.* Joly, 46f   On Malebranche's scientific work, consult further,

O Henry, *Malebranche d'après des manuscrits inédits la bibliothèque nationale*, *Revue Philosophique*, p 410 of Vol II, 1887

Lechelas, *L'oeuvre scientifique de Malebranche, Revue Philosophique*, 1884, p 293

P Duhem, *L'Optique de Malebranche, Revue de métaphysique et de morale*. Vol. XXIII, p. 37

[36] But *cf.* M Blondel, *L'Anti-cartésianisme de Malebranche, Revue de métaphysique et de morale*, Vol XXIII, p. 1   A very skillful comparison of Descartes and Malebranche is made in this article   The essential difference between the scientific spirit of Descartes and the religious spirit of Malebranche is brought out, the difference between "*méthode scientifique et rationale d'une part, méthode ascetique et speculative d'autre part*"   Cf 18ff   Bouillier, p 25.

[37] *Op. cit.*, Ed. of Jules Simon, Vol II, p 478.

[38] Bouillier, p 25

[39] Bouillier, p 26

[40] *Entretiens*, Ed of Jules Simon, p 95

of the world, he soon became famous through his writings, not only in France, but in foreign countries as well.[41] Fontanelle tells us that very few foreign *savants* came to Paris without visiting him.[42] Lord Quadrington, who died vice-regent of Jamaica, spent two or three hours every morning with Malebranche for two years studying his philosophy.[42] The Prince of Condé was an enthusiastic admirer.[42] Although of frail constitution, a severe manner of living gave him fairly good health throughout his life; he was seventy-seven years old, when in 1715, after an illness of four months, he was overtaken by death.[42]

Let us now turn to his doctrine.

[41] Bouillier, p 27
[42] Bouillier, p 28

CHAPTER II: MALEBRANCHE'S PSYCHOLOGY.

Cassirer has called attention to the psychological aspect of Malebranche's teaching. "The well known story," says this learned historian of the theory of knowledge, "which tells us that it was the reading of Descartes' *Traité de l'homme* that aroused Malebranche to his philosophical calling is very significant in this respect It is in fact from physiology, and from the physiological psychology which is necessarily connected with the former, that he takes his start. It is with this problem that he achieves his peculiar historical originality. . . . The analysis of the problem of perception led to results which precede and make possible the doctrine of Berkeley. Not the Englishmen, but Malebranche, is the first true psychologist in the history of modern philosophy."[1]

It is from this point of view that we can understand the structure of the *Recherche de la vérité*.[2] This work is an elaborate exposure of the errors to which the human mind is liable. Book I discusses the senses, Book II, the imagination, Book III, the pure understanding, Book IV, the inclinations, Book V, the passions, while, finally, Book VI deals with the general problem of scientific and philosophical method. All of these topics are discussed with regard to the problem of the *psychological* explanation of error. Malebranche thus combines the metaphysical theory of mind—the problem of the relation of mental and corporeal substances—with the empirically psychological consideration of mind. We shall later see how his great doctrine, that we see all things in God, is a necessary deduction from this dualistic metaphysics But for the present let us be content to trace our way through the *Recherche de la vérité*. We shall find that it possesses a peculiarly rich content from the psychological point of view As Bouillier exclaims "What a knowledge of the human heart, what profound and delicate observation, what portraits and characters of admirable *finesse* and striking truth, what piquant strokes in this description of all our mental ills!"[3] It is in this psychological regard that we shall first examine it. Later on we shall give more especial attention to the epistemological and metaphysical issues which Malebranche cannot refrain from discussing even in the *Recherche*.

[1] *Erkenntnisproblem*, Ed 2, Vol I p 554
[2] For the *Recherche de la vérité* I am using the Jules Simon edition
[3] Bouillier, p 89,

The Faculties of the Mind.

Let us consider, first of all, Book I, *Des sens.* Malebranche
begins with a general characterization of understanding and
will The human spirit is a simple and unextended being and
is in no way composed of parts. Nevertheless it is customary to
distinguish two faculties, understanding and will.[4] But these
ideas are very abstract and do not fall under the imagination,
it is, therefore, better to express them by a comparison with
matter, although, to be sure, this comparison with matter is not
"*entierement juste.*"[5] Matter possesses two faculties or properties; the first is that of receiving different figures, the second
is that of being moved. In the same way the human spirit has
two faculties: Understanding, which is the capacity of receiving ideas; the second, which is the will, is the capacity of receiving different inclinations or of willing different things.[5] Now
matter can receive two sorts of figures. One sort are entirely
exterior, like the roundness of a bit of wax; the other sort are
interior, like the figures of the minute parts of which the wax is
composed. The first are figures in the strict sense, the second
may be called configurations.[5] Now there are two sorts of perceptions of the soul which correspond to these two sorts of modifications of bodies; on the one hand we have pure perceptions
which may be considered as superficial to the soul, on the other
hand we have the more sensible perceptions, of which pleasure
and pain, light and color, taste and odor are examples Now.
says Malebranche, we shall see that these sensible perceptions
are nothing but modifications of the soul; thus as long as we do
not transcend sensible perceptions, we do not transcend the
states of our own consciousness.[6]

The faculty of receiving ideas and modifications, like the
capacity of matter of receiving both figures and configurations,
is entirely passive. In both cases we deal with a wholly receptive
faculty.[7] This theory of the essential passivity of understanding
plays an important role in Malebranche's epistemology. As
Bouillier has remarked, Malebranche's very use of a physical
analogy in his explanation of the nature of mind shows a tendency to deny the mind all activity and causal efficacy.[8] It would,
however, be well not to push this criticism too far.

The same analogy between the faculties of the mind and
the properties of matter holds in the case of will that holds in
the case of understanding.[9] Just as God is the cause of all the
movements of bodies so he is the cause of all the natural in-

[4] *Recherche,* I, p 2
[5] *Recherche,* I, p 3
[6] *Recherche,* I, p 4
[7] *Recherche,* I, p 5
[8] Bouillier, p 36
[9] *Recherche,* I, p 7.

clinations. In the same way that all movements take place in a straight line, if there are no foreign and special causes which determine them 'and change them into curves by their opposition; in the same way, all the inclinations that we have from God are "straight" (*droites*) and they would have no other end than the possession of the good and of the truth were there not a foreign cause that determines the impression of nature towards bad ends.[9] This special foreign factor is our freedom or liberty. Malebranche defines his terms as follows: "Hence by this word *Will*, I here designate the *impression*[10] or *natural movement which carries us toward the indeterminate and general good;* and by the word *Liberty* I understand nothing else than the *power which the mind has of turning this impression towards objects which please us, and thus bringing it about that our natural inclinations are directed upon some particular object,* while these inclinations were previously directed toward the good in general, or the universal good, that is to say, toward God, who is the sole general good, since it is he alone who includes within himself all goods."[11] Later he tells us that liberty is the power to compare goods and to love them in proportion as they are lovable and to relate them to the all-inclusive good, God.[12] Thus in the midst of a system which inclines toward an extreme absolutism, or over-emphasis of the omnipotence of God, we find Malebranche maintaining that the individual is yet in principle free.[13] In regard to the active side of mind, then, we may say that Malebranche regards it as a play of inclinations which have the divine being as both efficient and final cause—in terms of Aristotle's metaphysics—and yet as affording room for a certain spontaneity or liberty on the part of the mind itself.[14]

It will be remembered that Descartes regarded judgment as a function of will rather than of understanding. Judgment is an expression of free choice, otherwise the responsibility for human error would fall back upon the divine creator "Whereupon," says Descartes, "regarding myself more closely and considering what are my errors (for they alone testify to there being any imperfection in me) I answer that they depend on a combination of two causes, to-wit, on the faculty of knowledge that rests in me, and on the power of choice or of free will—that is to say, on the understanding and at the same time on the will For by the understanding alone I neither assert nor deny

---

[10] Malebranche uses this word as meaning *impetus* rather than *sensation*.

[11] *Recherche*, I, p. 8f   Cf Bouillier, pp 76, 77, 78

[12] *Recherche*, I, p 10

[13] As Bouillier has pointed out, Malebranche always endeavors to maintain the freedom of the individual, especially in the *Traité de la nature et de la grace* and in the *Traité de Morale*, Bouillier, p 79   Indeed, Arnauld, the Jansenist, accused Malebranche of Pelagianism, Bouillier, p. 79.   Nevertheless, says Bouillier, it is only by means of a grave contradiction that Malebranche admits freedom   Cf. Bouillier, p 80

[14] On this point, cf Ollé-Laprune, *La philosophie de Malebranche*, Vol I, p 287f

anything, but apprehend the ideas of things as to which I can
form a judgment But no error is properly speaking found in
it, provided the word error is taken in its proper signification.
. . . I likewise cannot complain that God has given me a free
choice or a will which is sufficient, ample, and perfect, since as
a matter of fact, I am conscious of a will so extended as to be
subject to no limitations. .   . From all this I recognize that
the power of will which I have received from God is not of itself
the source of my errors—for it is very ample and very perfect
of its kind—any more than is the power of understanding, for
since I understand nothing but by the power which God has
given me for understanding, there is no doubt that all I understand, I understand as I ought, and it is not possible that I err
in this. Whence then come my errors? They come from the
sole fact that since the will is much wider in its range and com-
pass than the understanding, I do not restrain it within the
same bounds, but extend it also to things which I do not understand, and as the will is of itself indifferent to these it easily
falls into error and sin and chooses the evil for the good, or the
false for the true.''[15] This element of voluntarism which thus
occurs in the heart of Descartes' rationalistic philosophy is also
found in Malebranche. ''The understanding merely perceives
and it is will alone that judges and reasons, in voluntarily rest-
ing in that which the understanding presents to it.''[16] It is by
painstaking critical analysis that any proposition comes to be
evident to us. When we have made it evident to ourselves, we
forget the effort or volitional activity that was necessary to
make it evident. But when there is something obscure in the
material under consideration, or when we have not made the
principles involved clear and logically transparent to ourselves,
then we are free to withhold our assent. It is this freedom to
doubt all that does not fully satisfy the intellect, all that is
not logically manifest, that is the basis of the possibility of true
knowledge. It is because we can doubt of that which is obscure
and ambiguous that we can elevate ourselves into the realm of
pure deductive truth. Thus this voluntaristic theory of judgment means, for both Descartes and Malebranche, in the first
place, the ability that the mind possesses of obtaining absolute,
logically coercive, truth. It is the opposite of any voluntaristic
theory of judgment that would reduce all truth to the arbitrary
choice of the individual. We may note that Spinoza, with perhaps greater clarity of vision, denies Descartes' notion that
judgment is an act of will, and declares in the *Ethics* that ''there
is in the mind no volition or affirmation and negation save that
which the idea, in so far as it is an idea, involves.''[17] That is,

[15] Meditation IV, *Philosophical Works of Descartes*, Trans. by Haldane and Ross,
Vol I, p 174
[16] *Recherche*, I, p 12. *Cf* Bouillier, p. 88f.
[17] *Ethics*, Part II, Prop XLIX.

the truth affirms itself in the mind without any arbitrary act of will. The note to this Proposition is a thorough criticism of the Cartesian and Malebranchian view. This liberty of the mind, *i. e.*, this ability to doubt all that is not logically coercive, is what renders potent the two maxims which are of central significance in Malebranche's system: (1) One should never give complete assent save to propositions which appear so evidently true that one cannot deny them without feeling an inner pain and the secret reproaches of reason;[18] and (2) One should never absolutely love a good if one can refrain from loving it without remorse.[18] It is on these rigorous maxims that Malebranche's system is founded. He sought a system of truth which would stand upon unyielding logical ground, and an object for his love that would maintain itself against all foreign attractions How closely he was here allying himself with Descartes is evident when we compare these maxims with those of Descartes' methodology. In the *Discourse on Method* Descartes lays down four rules of method of which the first is. ''To accept nothing as true which I do not clearly recognize to be so, that is to say, carefully to avoid precipitation and prejudice in judgments and to accept in them nothing more than what was presented to my mind so clearly and distinctly that I could have no occasion to doubt it ''[19] In this principle we have the basic idea from which all exact science springs, the criterion of logical coerciveness. We shall see how Malebranche's maxims unfold themselves in his philosophy as a whole.

The Senses.

But let us continue our account of Malebranche's psychology as expounded in the *Recherche* After the general and preliminary discussions which we have just reviewed, he enters upon a more detailed consideration of the errors which spring from the senses; here his psychology comes clearly to light. In the first place, we may note that Malebranche holds throughout to the theory that none of the sensible qualities are properties of external things themselves, but that they are all modifications of the mind itself.[20] The Tenth Chapter of the *Recherche*, Book I, establishes this point. It is true, he says, that the judgments that we make concerning extension, figure, and movement of bodies, involve some truth, but the same is not true in regard to light, color, taste, and all other sensible qualities, for here the truth is never met with.[21]

This theory Malebranche supports by reference to the metaphysical difference between mind and matter. He supposes that

---

[18] *Recherche*, I, p 17
[19] *Philosophical Works* Trans of Haldane and Ross, Vol I, p 92
[20] On this point *cf* Bouillier, pp 36-37, 88f
[21] *Recherche*, I, p 83

we are able to distinguish the soul from the body by positive
attributes and by the properties that belong to these two substances. Body is only extension in length, breadth, and depth
and all its properties are exhausted in rest and motion, and in
an infinity of different figures; for it is clear (1) that the idea
of extension represents a substance, since one can think of extension without thinking of anything else; and (2) that this idea
can only represent relations of distance, either successive or permanent, that is, either motions or figures The soul, on the contrary, is the ''I'' that thinks, that feels, that wills; it is the substance in which are found all the modifications of which I have
an inner feeling (*sentiment intérieur*) and which can only exist
in the soul that feels them.[22] Having laid down this fundamental metaphysical distinction, Malebranche proceeds as follows:
The sense-organs are composed of minute fibers which originate
in the brain, and extend hence into all our members and finally
end in the exterior parts of the body. If these nerve fibers are
externally stimulated, we have normal perception; if they are
internally stimulated, from the brain itself, we have the phenomena of dreams.[23] The final paragraph of this crucial chapter clarifies the whole doctrine by distinguishing four phases in
the process of perception. In the first place, we have the action
of the object, in the case of heat, for example, the movement of
the small particles of wood against the hand. Secondly, we
have the passion, or being acted upon of the organ of sense, for
example, the agitation of the fibers of the hand, which agitation
is communicated to the brain. Thirdly, we have the passion, or
sensation, of the soul, and, lastly, the judgment of the soul, by
which we place the sensation in its objective context.[24]

This last phase of the process is precisely where the illusion
of sense arises. For this judgment is merely a *jugement naturel*,
a *sensation composée*.[25] In other words, it is a natural belief
that holds that sensible qualities belong to external objects. Nevertheless, this natural or instinctive belief is not theoretically
trustworthy. The senses and our natural belief in the independent reality of their content are helpful from the standpoint
of the welfare of our bodies. They are pragmatically valuable.
The explanation of our habit of projecting our sensations into
an external world can ultimately only be on teleological grounds.
This explanation is given in Chapter XX, Book I, of the *Recherche*, but in more detail in the *Entretiens sur la métaphysique*. Thus, explains *Théodore*, in the latter, it is evident that
God, desiring to unite minds and bodies, had to establish as an
occasional cause of the confused knowledge we have of the pres-

[22] *Recherche*, I, p 84
[23] *Recherche*, I, p 85.
[24] *Recherche*, I, p 90.
[25] *Recherche*, I, p 90

ence of objects and of their properties in relation to us, not our attention, which merits clear and distinct knowledge, but various disturbances of these same bodies. He had to give us distinct witnesses, not of the nature and properties of the bodies that surround us, but of the relation which they bear to our own body, that we can work with success for the conservation of life, without being incessantly attentive to our needs. He had to give us short proofs of that which has reference to the body, to convince us promptly with vivid proofs that would effectively determine us, with sure proofs that no one would think of contradicting, in order the more surely to preserve us. But these proofs are essentially confused in character and are certain not with regard to the relations between objects, in which consists truth, but with regard to our bodies in their actual disposition [26] It is the divine foresight that explains the persistent and universal illusion in which the mass of mankind grope, for it is by means of this illusion that we find our way through the world of bodies.

But let us return to our study of the psychology of the *Recherche*. It is this objectification of sensible qualities that is the greatest error arising from sense.[27] But Malebranche does not rest here. Our sense of sight perpetually deceives us as to the size of objects, and is blind to everything smaller than a certain size. It is essentially inexact.[28] It is from the senses that there arises the false philosophy of scholasticism.[29]

Let us assume that sensible qualities exist in bodies themselves Then it is indubitable that what I sense in honey differs essentially from what I sense in salt. The whiteness of salt differs beyond doubt more than merely in degree from the color of honey, and the sweetness of honey differs in the same way from th piquant taste of salt. Consequently, according to this argument, it is necessary that there be an essential difference between honey and salt; since everything that I sense in the one does not differ merely as a matter of more or less from what I sense in the other, but differs in essence. Since then honey and salt and other natural bodies differ essentially from each other, it follows that they deceive themselves who try to make us believe that the whole difference that is found between bodies consists in differences of configuration of the small bodies that compose them. It is necessary then that some other substance be found that, being joined to the primary matter which is common to all bodies, bring it about that they differ essentially from each other. This will be the second step and the discovery of *substantial forms*, those fecund substances which produce every-

[26] *Entretiens*, p 85   Jules Simon edition
[27] *Cf.* Joly, p 215ff
[28] *Recherche*, I, pp. 42 69
[29] *Recherche*, I, pp 125-134

thing that we see in nature and that only exist in the imagination of the philosopher.[30] Thus arises the whole medieval world of substances, essences, and substantial forms. It rests upon the illusion of the objective and independent existence of sensible qualities. In this Malebranche has laid his finger upon the radical difference between the medieval system of the universe and that explained in modern science. On the one hand reliance is placed on the immediate appearance of things to the senses; on the other, upon pure mathematics together with critically analyzed experience.[31]

The senses are the source, not only of theoretical illusions, but of moral illusions as well. The excessive attention that the mass of mankind give to sensuous good comes from the same source. We believe that "all those agreeable tastes which delight us at feasts, those sounds which flatter the ear, and those other pleasures that we feel are, undoubtedly, contained in the sensible objects, or at least these objects cause us to feel them."[32] The truth is, in terms of Malebranche's system, that sensuous objects neither contain the pleasures nor produce them; they are contained in the soul as its modifications and are produced by the one truly efficient cause in the universe, the divine will.[33] The error of the Epicureans consists in just this: That they regard sensible things as the causes of our pleasures and as therefore worthy of love.[34] The error of Stoicism rests on the same assumption. They place pleasures and pains in the outer objects and insist that the soul should seek its own good. They thus reach the false conclusion that pain is not an evil, nor pleasure a good. The true ethical point of view comes to light only when we regard pleasures and pains as states of the soul itself, and as flowing from the one supreme good, the divine being.

These remarks may suffice to give us a notion of Malebranche's psychology of the senses and of his theory of the illusion-generating character of the same.[35] Like Plato he believed that the first requisite for profound philosophical and scientific views was distrust of the senses and of all the information they offer, and confidence in the ability of pure thought to master the world.

The Imagination.

Let us now examine his critique of imagination.

This fills the second book of the *Recherche*.[36] Malebranche begins by distinguishing the faculties of imagination and sense from the point of view of physiological psychology. The agitation of the minute fibers of the nerves cannot pass to the brain

[30] *Recherche*, I, p. 127
[31] *Cf.* Cassirer, *Erkenntnisproblem*, I, p 203ff and many other places
[32] *Recherche*, I, p 130
[33] *Recherche*, I, p. 132
[34] *Recherche*, I, p 133
[35] Bouillier, pp 86-87.
[36] On Malebranche's doctrine of imagination *cf* Bouillier, p 90

without the soul perceiving something, if the agitation commences by an impression that an object makes on the exterior surface of our nerve fibers, the soul feels and judges that what she feels is outside, that is, that she perceives an object as present But if only the inner fibers are agitated by the movements of the animal spirits, or in some other manner, the soul imagines, and judges that what she imagines is not without but within the brain, that is, she perceives an object as absent.[37] Imagination is akin to sense-perception The difference is a difference in vivacity.[37] Two phases of imagination may be distinguished, the active and the passive. The first is under control of the will, the second is more under control of the animal spirits and the fibers of the brain.[38] - "Imagination, then," says Malebranche, "consists solely in the power that the soul possesses of forming images of objects, by imprinting them in the brain; the stronger and more distinct the vestiges of the animal spirits are the more distinctly and strongly will the soul imagine its objects."[39] It is the difference in the force of the animal spirits and the definiteness of their imprint on the brain that explains the observable difference in the imaginations of different men.[39] Malebranche proceeds-to point out the various factors that can influence the imagination. Wine is one of the first agencies mentioned Malebranche quotes Horace:

> *Quid non ebrietas designat? operta recludit:*
> *Spes jubet esse ratas: in praelia trudit inermem*
> *Sollicitis animis onus eximit: addocet artis.*
> *Fecundi calices quem non fecere disertum,*
> *Contracta quem non in paupertate solutum?*[40]

The air that one breathes has an influence on the imagination This is manifest in the different mental characteristics of persons of different countries. The Gascons, for example, have a much more vivid imagination than the Normans. People of Rouen and of Dieppe and the Picardians all differ from each other, and still more from the Low Normans, although they are sufficiently close to each other. But if we consider men who live in more widely separated countries, we meet still greater differences, such as those between an Italian, a Fleming and a Dutchman. And lastly there are places renowned in all times for the wisdom of their inhabitants, like Therma and Athens; and other places are renowned for stupidity, like Thebes and Abdera [41] The imagination is affected by the nerves that go to the heart and lungs, viscera, etc. Each image is correlated

---

[37] *Recherche*, I, p 151   Cf Bouillier, p. 40f
[38] *Recherche*, I p 152
[39] *Recherche*, I p 153
[40] *Recherche*, I p 158
[41] *Recherche*, I, p. 162

with a *"trace du cerveau,"* with a cerebral trace, and memory is to be explained by the mutual connection between these cerebral traces. To understand memory, according to Malebranche, it is sufficient to understand this truth. "That all our different perceptions are attached to changes that take place in the principal part of the brain in which the soul more especially resides. . . . For, in the same way that the branches of a tree, which have remained bent in a certain fashion for some time, retain some facility for being bent again in the same manner, so the fibers of the brain, having once received impressions from the movements of the animal spirits and the action of objects, retain for a long time a facility for receiving these same dispositions. Now memory consists only in this facility, since one only thinks of the same things when the brain receives the same impressions." In very s i m i l a r terms, Malebranche explains habit.[42]

It does not fall within the purpose of this study to follow Malebranche's psychology of imagination into its details. We may note, however, discussions of the "communication between the brain of a mother and that of her (unborn) child,"[43] of "changes that take place in the imagination of a child in issuing from the womb of his mother, by conversation with its nurse, its mother, and other persons."[44]

Several chapters are devoted to the various types of imagination. These chapters reveal the keen analyst of human nature. Of women he says: "It is for them to decide as to the fashions, to judge as to language, to discern the correct air and fine manners. They have more knowledge, skill, and *finesse* than men concerning such things. Whatever depends on taste is in their field, but ordinarily they are incapable of penetrating to truths a little difficult of discovery. Whatever is abstract is incomprehensible to them. They cannot avail themselves of their imagination to develop complicated and embarrassed questions. . . . In short, the manner and not the reality is enough to exhaust the capacity of their minds, because the least objects produce great movements in the delicate fibers of their brains, and consequently necessarily excite in their souls feelings sufficiently vivacious and great enough to occupy them completely."[45] Of course, Malebranche is obliged to admit that there may be exceptions to this generalization There are *femmes savantes*, courageous women, women capable of everything, and there can be found, on the other hand, men who are soft and effeminate, incapable of understanding anything and incapable

---

[42] *Recherche,* I, p 182ff Cf Joly, p 225ff
[43] *Recherche,* I, p 189
[44] *Recherche,* I, p 212
[45] *Recherche,* I, p 222

of doing anything.[46] A man's mind is at its prime between the
ages of thirty and fifty. Then his cerebral fibers are of the right
consistency; sufficiently firm to assure intellectual self-mastery,
and not so firm as to prevent all new forms of cerebral modification.[47] But men are not only confirmed in their views when
they have reached the age of forty or fifty years. They are
subject to new errors; they believe themselves capable of judging of everything, as indeed they ought to be. They decide with
presumption and consult only their prejudices, for men do not
reason of things save by relation to the ideas that are the most
familiar to them. A peripatetic thinks first of the four elements
and the four qualities, while a philosopher of another school re-
lates everything to other principles.[48] As is explained at length[49]
the animal spirits ordinarily flow in the traces of the most familiar ideas, which brings it about that we do not judge sanely
of things.

Studious persons are especially subject to error.[50] They are
lovers of authority. It is difficult to understand, says Malebranche, how it happens that people who have minds prefer to
use the minds of others in the search for truth rather than the
mind that God gave them. There is beyond doubt infinitely more
pleasure and honor in guiding oneself by one's own eyes than
by those of others; and a man who has good eyes would never
think of closing them or of tearing them out in the hope of having a guide. *Sapientis oculi, in capite ejus, stultus in tenebris
ambulat.* Why does the fool walk in darkness? It is because
he only sees by the eyes of others and to see only in this manner
is properly speaking not to see at all. The use of the mind is
to the use of the eyes what the mind is to the eyes, as the mind
is infinitely higher than the eyes, so the use of the mind is accompanied by much more solid satisfactions and by a very different contentment than light and colors afford sight. Men,
however, always avail themselves of their eyes to guide themselves, and very rarely avail themselves of their minds to discover truth.[51]

Malebranche suggests a number of causes of this natural
weakness of the mind. In the first place we have man's natural laziness. Secondly, the inability of men in meditation
owing to lack of practice in youth, when the cerebral fibers are
plastic. Thirdly, man's lack of love for abstract truth, which
is the foundation of all that we can know *ici-bas.* Fourthly,
our love of pleasant and sensible probabilities, mere casual plaus-

[46] *Recherche,* I, p 223
[47] *Recherche,* I, p 225
[48] *Recherche,* I, p 226
[49] *Recherche,* I, p 230-234.
[50] *Recherche,* I, p. 235
[51] *Recherche,* I, p 237

ibilities   Fifthly, our stupid vanity which makes us desire to
appear learned, for they are called learned who have read the
most.   Sixthly, we imagine, without reason, that the ancients
were more enlightened than we can be, and that where they
have failed no one can succeed.   Seventhly, because of a false
reverence mixed with a stupid curiosity as to distant things, old
things, things that come from afar or from unknown countries,
or from obscure books.   Eighthly, because when we admire a
new opinion and a new author we are afraid that their fame
will outshine our own, while one has nothing to fear when one
pays homage to the ancients.   In the ninth place, it is falsely
believed that because it is wrong to make innovations in religious faith, it is wrong to make changes in science.   A tenth
cause of undue conservatism in science and philosophy is the
fact that we live in a time in which the knowledge of ancient
opinions is in vogue and few can rise above what is customary.
And lastly, because men act only according to their interests,
and even those who perceive the error and vanity of their ways
do not cease to apply themselves to these same studies because
of the honors and dignities that are attached to them.   This
"terrific" attack on the spirit of scholasticism and of erudition
was characteristic of Malebranche.   He loved the pure truths
of reason, the eternal ideas in the mind of God, so well that he
had little use for the truths of history and scholarship.   He develops the same theme in chapters on "Two bad effects of reading."[52]   "That people ordinarily grow stubborn, concerning
whom their aim is to know what he said without caring as to
what they should believe."[53]   Another chapter is "On the pre-
occupation of commentators."[54]   It is refreshing to a historical
student to find at last an equally penetrating paragraph on "The
invention on new systems," in which it comes to light that nov-
elty is not always preferable.[55]

Malebranche's analysis of the psychology of imagination is
so penetrating that it is difficult not to examine it more completely than considerations of time and space permit us in the
present study.[56]   A special division of the book of the *Recherche*
on Imagination is devoted to the contagious communication of
strong imaginations.   Strong imaginations are extremely influential and dominate weaker imaginations.   Thus those who have
strong and vigorous imaginations are very frequently the cause
of the general errors that are spread among mankind.[57]   God
has united the human race by certain natural bonds, which con-

[52] *Recherche*, I, p 241
[53] *Recherche*, I, p 245
[54] *Recherche*, I, p. 252
[55] *Recherche*, I, p. 262
[56] Cf Bouillier, p 94
[57] *Recherche*, I, p. 278

sist in a certain disposition of men to imitate those with whom
they converse, to make the same judgments and enter into the
same passions with them.[58] This disposition to imitate has itself two causes. The first is the desire for a high place in the
opinions of others; the second cause of the disposition to imitate is this influence exerted by stronger imaginations over
weaker imaginations.[59]

Malebranche distinguishes a strong as opposed to a weak
imagination in terms of cerebral structure. He has a strong
and vigorous imagination whose brain has a constitution which
renders it capable of extremely deep vestiges and traces.[60] An
imagination of this sort is capable of so completely occupying
the soul that it can think of nothing save the images presented
by this imagination.[61] People endowed with strong imaginations in this sense are not capable of judging sanely of complicated things. The capacity of their minds is exhausted by ideas
which are connected with deep cerebral traces, and they are
not at liberty to think of many things at the same time.[62] These
people are always visionaries. They are always in excess; they
elevate unworthy things, magnify small things, make distant
things seem near.[63] Nothing appears to them as it is. They are
vehement in their passions, obstinate in their opinions, always
satisfied with themselves.[63] They have great facility in talking
in a manner that is strong and vivid although not natural Their
thoughts, being connected with deep cerebral traces, are accompanied by vivid emotion [64] The look of their countenances, the
tone of their voices, and the turn of their words animate their
expressions and cause those who hear them to be attentive and
to receive mechanically their ideas. When a man is penetrated
with what he has to say, he penetrates others, and an impas-
sioned man always moves those who hear him. Persons of this
sort of imagination ordinarily speak only of easy subjects that
are within the reach of every one, they only treat of great and
difficult matters in a vague and commonplace way, without ven-
turing to enter into detail and without attaching themselves to
principles. Such people are ordinarily the enemies of reason
and of good sense by reason of the pettiness of their minds and
of the visions to which they are subject.[65]

The influence of imagination over imagination is seen in
the case of children and parents, daughters and mothers, serv-

[58] *Recherche*, I, p. 279
[59] *Recherche*, I, p 280
[60] *Recherche*, I, p. 281
[61] *Recherche*, I, p 281.
[62] *Recherche*, I, p 283
[63] *Recherche*, I, p 285.
[64] *Recherche*, I, p. 286
[65] *Recherche*, I, p 288

ants and masters, pupils and teachers, courtiers and kings.[66]
But it comes clearly to light in the influence of great authors.
And here Malebranche displays again keen and vivid insight.
His characterizations of the relatively small number of authors
with whom he was familiar are admirable. Tertullian, he says,
was in truth a man of profound erudition, but he had more
memory than judgment, more penetration and extent of imagination than penetration and extent of intellect.[67] The imagination of Seneca was no better ordered than that of Tertullian to
carry him into a country that is unknown to him, where nevertheless he moves with the same assurance that he would have if
he knew where he was and where he was going. Provided he
makes great strides, and strides in regular cadence, he imagines
that he is greatly advancing, but he is like those who, in danc-
ing, always finish where they began.[68] Montaigne is not to be
regarded as a man who reasons but as a man who amuses himself, as a man who tries to please rather than to instruct. If
those who read him could merely amuse themselves with him,
he would not be injurious; but the mind cannot draw pleasure
from the reading of an author without imitating his feelings
It is not only dangerous to read Montaigne because of the pleasure one is insensibly led to take in his sentiments, but because
this pleasure is criminal, for it is born of concupiscence and does
nothing but fortify the passions.[69] The easy skepticism of Montaigne, with its worldly point-of view, was thus deeply repug-
nant to the Oratorian

This remarkable portrayal of the secret workings of the
imagination terminates in the injunction to seek to deliver ourselves from the illusions of sense and imagination, and from the
illusions generated by the imaginations of other men in our
minds. Let us reject with care all the confused ideas that we
have by reason of our dependence on our bodies and only admit
the clear and evident ideas that the spirit receives from the
union that it necessarily has with the Word (*Logos*), or eternal
wisdom and truth.[70] Malebranche's psychological insight has
that clarity and profundity that are the natural right of the
meditative man, who lives, perhaps, more or less as a recluse,
and yet perceives in his own self the universal motives of human life.[71]

Our Lack of an Idea of the Soul.

The Third Book of the *Recherche* is on the "Understanding
or Pure Spirit " The major part of this discussion we shall

[66] *Recherche*, I, p 289
[67] *Recherche*, I, p 301
[68] *Recherche*, I, p 304
[69] *Recherche*, I, p 319
[70] *Recherche*, p 388
[71] Cf *Joly* p 222.

consider later under the head of Theory of Knowledge. There
is but one point that here deserves attention. And to understand this point we must turn again to Descartes. In the doctrine of the *cogito ergo sum* the consciousness of thought of its
own activity is made the starting-point of philosophy. Our
clearest idea is an idea of our self. In the *Principles of Philosophy,* for example, Descartes explains "How we may know
our mind better than our body." "But," he says, "in order to
understand how the knowledge which we possess of our mind
not only precedes that which we have our body but is also more
evident, it must be observed that it is very manifest by the natural light which is in our souls, that no qualities or properties
pertain to nothing; and that where some are perceived there
must necessarily be some thing or substance on which they depend. And the same light shows us that we know a thing or
substance so much the better the more properties we observe
in it. And we certainly observe many more qualities in our
mind than in any other thing, inasmuch as there is nothing
that excites us to knowledge of whatever kind which does not
even more certainly compel us to a consciousness of our thought.
To take an example, if I persuaded myself that there is an earth
because I touch or see it, by that very same fact and by a yet
stronger reason, I should be persuaded that my thought exists,
because it may be that I think I touch the earth even though
there is possibly no earth existing at all, but it is not possible
that I who form this judgment and my mind which judges thus,
should be non-existent; and so in other cases '"[72] The soul is
thus its own clearest object.

Now Malebranche holds that although we have a superior
consciousness of the *existence* of the soul as compared to our
consciousness of the *existence* of matter, we have on the other
hand a superior consciousness of the *essence* of matter as compared to our consciousness of the essence of the soul. We are
more certain *that* the soul is than *that* the body is; but we are
more certain as to *what* the body is than as to *what* the soul is.
Malebranche does not believe, as he tells us, that after having
given the matter serious thought it is possible to doubt that the
essence of the mind consists in thought, in the same way that
the essence of matter consists in extension; and that according
to different modifications of thought the mind now wills and
now imagines, or assumes other particular forms, in the same
way as, according to different modifications of extension, matter
is now water, now wood, now fire or has some other of an infinity
of possible particular forms.[73] Thus we are capable of knowing
that the essence of mind is thought, but only in a general way.

[72] *Philosophical Works*, Haldane and Ross, Vol I, p 223

[73] *Recherche*, I, p 341

We do not possess the "idea" of the soul.[74] We do not behold the soul in God.[74] We only know the soul by *conscience*, by *sentiment intérieur*, that is, by inner experience.[75] For that reason the knowledge we have of it is imperfect. Had we never felt pain, heat, light, etc., we should not know that our soul was capable of these feelings. Were it true, on the contrary, that we beheld in God the idea of our soul, we should be able to deduce from it all the properties of which it is capable, just as we can deduce from the idea of extension all the modifications it is capable of assuming.[74] If we knew nothing of matter save some twenty or thirty figures we should know practically nothing; we may say that we are capable of knowing the nature of matter because we can evolve an infinity of mathematical forms out of the idea of extension. But we have no deductive knowledge of the possible modifications of the soul. Nevertheless, adds Malebranche, our *sentiment intérieur* demonstrates the Immortality, Spirituality and Liberty of the soul.[75]

This same point is made in the *Entretiens*. Théodore urges that some truth must be contained in our mental states as mental states. "For it is a truth that I now have much joy in listening to you. It is true that the pleasure that I feel at present is greater than that which I felt in our preceding conversations. I know, then, the difference between these two pleasures. And I do not know it otherwise than by the feeling (*sentiment*) that I have of it, by the modalities with which my soul is affected; modalities, then, which are not so dark that they do not teach me a constant truth." *Ariste* replies: "You should say, Théodore, that you feel this difference in your modalities and in your pleasures. But do not say, if you please, that you *know* it God knows it and does not feel it. But as for you, you feel it without knowing it. If you had a clear idea of your soul, if you saw the archetype of it, then you would know that which you now only feel."[76] And *Ariste* goes on to point out the unmeasurable character of mental facts, urging that if we were really to know them it would be necessary to know them mathematically.

[74] *Recherche*, I, p 413

[75] *Recherche*, I, p 415 Cf *Bouillier*, p 57f. Bouillier holds that Malebranche and Gassendi agree on the obscurity of our knowledge of the soul, but that they reach this identical result by different methods Gassendi was over-occupied with the sensible, Malebranche with the divine Bouillier, *idem* As Bouillier points out, Malebranche thought that God did not permit us to behold the idea of the soul lest we be so occupied with its beauty that we forget everything else (*Meditation, X*) Bouillier, p 58 Victor Delbos has made an interesting comparison of Malebranche and Maine de Biran "On conçoit," says Delbos, "que sur cette affirmation du caratere irréductible et singulier de la donnée de conscience, tout en l'estimant incomplete, Maine de Biran ait pu sympathiser avec Malebranche" See *Revue de métaphysique et du morale* Vol XXIII, *Malebranche et Maine de Biran*, p 157

[76] *Entretiens*, p 113

We may note that this doctrine of Malebranche's has been compared with the theory of Hume that we have no logical basis for belief in a permanent self. Dr. C. W. Doxsee[77] compares Malebranche's position that "we do not see the soul in God" and that "we only know of our soul what we feel taking place within us," to Hume's statement that "when I enter most intimately into myself I always stumble upon some particular perception or other, of heat or cold, of light or shade, love or hatred, pain or pleasure." Dr. Doxsee declares· "Now this argument from introspection is common to both Hume and Malebranche and is really fundamentally one in both. They are at one in recognizing that 'inner sense' is totally unable to reveal the existence of a simple abiding spiritual substance behind the phenomena of consciousness."[78] It is hardly to be denied that this comparison is somewhat misleading. For the standards of knowability employed by Malebranche and Hume respectively differ completely. Malebranche says that we have no knowledge of the soul because we cannot give a mathematical or deductive explication of the idea, because we cannot deduce its modifications from it; Hume, on the contrary, rejects the idea of the self because he can find no impression from which it could be derived. There is a similarity in their results, but a radical difference in their methods of reaching those results. Furthermore, Malebranche would never have admitted that "inner sense is totally unable to reveal the existence of a simple abiding spiritual substance."[79] The very sentence quoted by Doxsee from Malebranche proves the contrary: "We only know of our soul by what we feel taking place within us."

[77] *Philosophical Review*, Vol XXV, p 704
[78] Doxsee, *idem*
[79] Doxsee, *idem*

CHAPTER III· MALEBRANCHE'S PSYCHOLOGY (Continued).

The Natural Inclinations.

Let us continue our account of Malebranche's psychology. The Fourth Book of the *Recherche de la vérité* concerns the "Inclinations or Natural Passions of the Mind."[1] Just as God gave motion to matter, so he gave inclinations to minds.[2] But it is an incontestable truth that God has no end for his actions but himself.[3] He must have himself as his principal end, for he would err were he to put his end in everything that did not, like himself, contain all good[3] Nevertheless, he can have, as a subordinate end, the conservation of created beings, for these too, to a certain extent, can participate in his goodness. Now the natural inclinations of created minds are certainly continual impressions of the will of their creator and conserver.[3] It is necessary that they can have no other principal end than his glory, nor secondary end than their own conservation and the conservation of others, but always with regard to him who gave them being.[4] There is, strictly speaking, in God only one love, which is love of himself, and as God can love nothing save by that love, since God can love nothing save by relation to himself, thus God has given us only one love, which is the love of good in general.[4] Love of the good in general is the principle of all our special loves.[4] This love is our will, which is simply the continual impression exerted by God on all finite creatures towards the all-inclusive good.[5]

Not only does our will for good in general come from God, our inclinations for particular goods, which are common in all men, such as our inclination for the perpetuation of our own being and of those with whom we are united by nature, are simply effects of the divine will as exerted upon us[6] This inclination for the good in general is the cause of the inquietude of our will, for striving for a universal good necessarily gives the soul a continual agitation. Whatever the mind regards as a particular good is finite, and the finite can only attract the will for a time; it cannot permanently hold it[7] The will is always restless; it is forced to seek what it cannot find; hence, it loves what

---

[1] On this subject *cf* Ollé-Laprune, *La philosophie de Malebranche*, Vol I, p 296ff
[2] *Recherche*, II, p 1
[3] *Recherche*, II, p 3
[4] *Recherche*, II, p 4
[5] *Cf* Ollé Laprune, *La philosophie de Malebranche* Vol I p 30ff
[6] *Recherche*, II, p 5
[7] *Recherche*, II, p 8

is great or extraordinary, whatever is like the infinite.[8] Not having found its good among common and familiar things, the mind seeks it in the unknown. Now this restlessness of the will is a great cause of illusion, and is thus related to Malebranche's central purpose in writing the *Recherche*, the exposure of the psychological causes of error. The will is generally more concerned with our happiness than with truth.[8] The essential restlessness of the will prevents sufficient application to any one subject.[8] This explains why the principles of morality are so little understood,[9] and why the truths of religion had to be made evident to the senses through revelation rather than discovered by reason.[10]

With unwearied thoroughness, Malebranche points out the relation between our inclinations and our errors. All the secret machinations of self-love and vanity are laid bare. The sections, "On the desire to appear wise," "On the conversations of false *savants*," "How our inclination for dignities and wealth leads to error," are complete and adequate discussions of their subjects. But there is no need for us in this study to follow this analysis into its details. It is enough for us to appreciate its general character.[11]

The Passions.

The Fifth Book of the *Recherche* is on the Passions. It opens with a masterly definition. The human mind has two essential relations, one to the body, the other to God. As pure spirit, man is essentially united with the Word of God, eternal wisdom and truth, sovereign reason.[12] But as human spirit, man is united to the body. In sense or imagination the mind has the body as the occasional cause of its modifications, and in understanding it is directly united with God. Now it is the same with the human will. As pure will it depends essentially on the love that God bears to himself. But as human will it is related to the body. "Natural inclinations" is the proper term for all the movements of the soul which we have in common with pure intelligences; "passions" is to be applied to all the emotions the soul feels on the occasion of extraordinary movements of animal spirits and the blood. It is thus the addition of a bodily element that distinguishes the passions from the inclinations. Descartes, in his *Passions of the Soul*[13] defines the passions as "the perceptions, feelings or emotions of the soul which

---

[8] *Recherche*, II, p. 9

[9] *Recherche*, II, p 10

[10] *Recherche*, II, p. 13

[11] But *cf.* Bouillier, p 97ff, and Joly, p 109ff

[12] *Recherche*, II, p 129

[13] Cf D Irons, *Descartes and Modern Theories of Emotion*, Philosophical Review, Vol IV, p 291

relate especially to it, and which are caused, maintained, and fortified by some movement of the (animal) spirits.''[14] And further on in the same treatise he explains that "they (the passions) are principally caused by the (animal) spirits which are contained in the cavities of the brain, in as much as they take their course towards the nerves which serve to enlarge or contract the orifices of the heart, or to drive in various ways to it the blood which is in other parts, or, in whatever other fashion it may be, to carry on the same passion, we may from this clearly understand why I have placed in my definition of them above, that they are caused by some particular movement of the animal spirits ''[15] In laying stress upon a physical factor as the *differentia* of passion Malebranche is thus carrying on the thought of Descartes.

The most complete analysis of passion occurs in Book V, Chapter III, of the *Recherche*. Malebranche holds that in each passion, with the exception of admiration, seven phases can be distinguished. (1) First we have an intellectual judgment, or either clear or confused view of the relation the object bears to us [16] (2) Then we have the movement of the will towards the object; previously to the just-mentioned judgment the will was directed merely towards the good in general. But when the mind perceives this relation of the object to it, a movement of the will occurs.[16] (3) Then we have in each of the passions a "sentiment" or feeling, such as love, aversion, desire, joy, sadness. These feelings are different in each of the different passions. (4) This is followed by a new determination of the course of the animal spirits and of the blood towards the exterior parts of the body. The animal spirits are forced into the muscles of the arms, of the face, and of all the outer parts of the body to put them in a condition appropriate to the dominating passion. If the forces of the individual are not sufficient to fulfill his need, his animal spirits are mechanically distributed in such a way as to cause him to utter certain words and cries and to assume a certain posture of countenance and body of a nature to attract the attention of others who may be able to help him. In this way the human species is bound together [17] (5) We then have a sensible emotion of the soul. This is the necessary psychic accompaniment of the disturbance of the animal spirits.[17] (6) We now have the feelings of love, of aversion, of joy, of desire or of sadness. This is distinct from the purely intellectual feeling described in (3), for it includes the expression of the disturbances of the animal spirits.[18] (7) Lastly, we have a certain feeling of

---

[14] *Philosophical Works*, Ross and Haldane, Vol I, p 344

[15] *Op cit*, Vol I, p 348

[16] *Recherche*, II, p. 147

[17] *Recherche*, II, p. 150

[18] *Recherche*, II, p 151

joy, of *douceur intérieur,* which stops the soul in its passion and witnesses to it that the soul is now in the state it should be in in regard to the object it is considering   This *douceur intérieur* accompanies generally all the passions, those which spring from the sight of evil as well as those which come from the sight of good.[18]   This *douceur* is what renders all our passions agreeable to us, and it is this *douceur* that must be conquered by the *douceur* of reason and faith, if we are to be freed from slavery to passions directed toward sensible goods.[18]   This analysis of passion, which one can only characterize as masterly, is further elaborated in the same chapter.   The limits of the present study alone prevent presentation of this elaboration.

Chapters IV and V do not require analysis here.   Their titles, "That the pleasures and movements of the passions involve us in error in regard to the good, and that they must be perpetually resisted," and "That the perfection of the mind consists in its union with God by knowledge of the truth and love of virtue; and, on the contrary, that its imperfection comes from its dependence on the body by reason of the disorders of sense and passion," indicate, as a perusal of their contents verifies, that they fall rather in the realm of ethics than in that of psychology.   But in the remaining chapters we find much valuable material   The most general error of sense is that we project our sensations into the outer world and regard them as independently existing properties of objects; the general error that comes from the passions is of the same sort.[19]   We attribute to the objects that cause them all the disturbances of our hearts, our good will, our gentleness, our malice, our anger and all the other qualities of our minds.   When we love some person we tend to believe that this person loves us, and we can scarcely conceive that he should have the design of destroying us, or of opposing himself to our desires.   But if hatred succeeds love, we cannot believe that this person wishes us well; we are always on our guard and defiant, although the person in question may not be even thinking of us or is thinking only of rendering us some service.[20]   Our passions not only disguise their principal objects, but all things that are related to them.   They not only render amiable all the qualities of our friends, but even the greater part of the qualities of the friends of our friends.[21]

With this as a point of departure, Malebranche discusses "Admiration and its bad effects,"[22] "The good uses one can make of admiration and of the other passions,"[23] "Love and

[18] *Recherche,* II, p 134
[20] *Recherche,* II, p 185
[21] *Recherche,* II, p 187
[22] *Recherche,* II, p 191f.
[23] *Recherche,* II, p 215f

aversion,''[24] ''That the passions all justify themselves,''[25] and ''That those passions which have evil as an object are the most dangerous and the most unjust, and that those which are accompanied with least knowledge are the most vivid and sensible.''[26] Space is lacking here for any fair treatment of the content of these chapters; it may be said, however, in a general way, that they merely carry through the general principles we have already made clear.[27]

[24] *Recherche*, II, p. 225f.

[25] *Recherche*, II, p. 240f.

[26] *Recherche*, II, p. 250f.

[27] *Cf.* Bouillier, p. 100f, and Joly, p. 230f. Most modern psychologists, I presume, would agree with the general judgment on Malebranche by Van Bièma. ''Malebranche montre donc une grand indépendence d'esprit lorsque la religion n'est pas en jeu. Il pouvait utiliser avec fruit ses belles qualités de psychologue; il aime à analyser la vie de l'esprit, les perceptions, les émotions, les inclinations, à rechercher les consequences de l'imagination ou des passions, on connâit sa finesse de 'moraliste.' . . . Mais d'abord la psychologie n'a jamais été pour lui qu'un moyen, elle se subordonne à la logique et à la morale. Et surtout il avait une connaisance trop précise de la nature de Dieu, de ses perfections, de ses volontés. Une métaphysique aussi audacieuse et aussi sûre d'elle-même est bien dangereuse pour un savant.'' *Revue de Métaphysique et du Morale*, Vol. XXIII, p. 127f. The citation is from p. 146.

CHAPTER IV: MALEBRANCHE'S THEORY OF KNOWLEDGE

We now take up Malebranche's most famous doctrine ⟨*That
we see all things in God*⟩ For in this proposition is summed up
his specific contribution to the Theory of Knowledge. We take
as our primary authority Part II of Book III of the *Recherche*,
correcting and supplementing this authority where necessary
with material drawn from other sources.

The Argument for Vision in God.

Every one will agree, says Malebranche, that we do not perceive objects outside of us by themselves. We see the sun, the
stars and an infinity of outer objects. But it is not probable
that the soul leaves the body and goes, so to speak, marching
through the skies to contemplate objects seen there. The soul
does not see them in themselves; the immediate object of our
mind when it beholds the sun, for example, is not the sun, but
something that is intimately united with the mind, and may be
called the idea of the sun. By idea, Malebranche understands,
in the first place, the immediate object of the mind.[1] When the
mind perceives something, or believes that it perceives something,
it is absolutely necessary that there actually be an idea whether
or not there exists any object of this idea.[2]

Men naturally believe that corporeal things are more real
than ideas; they think that the existence of corporeal things is
assured in spite of the fact that it often happens that our ideas
have nothing external to correspond to them, and it is certain
that external things do not resemble ideas.[2] Men regard the
idea as nothing, just as if ideas did not have a great many properties, as if the idea of a square and of any given number were
not essentially different, a thing which could not possibly be true
if ideas were "nothings."[2] If then ideas are *"très-réelle,"* let
us inquire into their nature.

All the things perceived by the soul are of two kinds: either
they are within the soul or they are without.[3] Those that are
within the soul are its own modifications, and may be expressed
by *pensée, manière de penser, modification de l'âme.*[3] Under this
head we may consider the sensations, imaginations, intellections,
conceptions, passions and natural inclinations.[3] The soul has
no need of ideas to perceive these things in the way it does perceive them; but it needs ideas to perceive external things[3] It is

[1] *Recherche*, I, p 373
[2] *Recherche*, I, p 374
[3] *Recherche*, I, p 375

possible that in the case of beings higher than man, such as the
angels, direct perception of spirit by spirit is possible without
the intermediation of ideas; thus ideas are only absolutely necessary in the case of the perception of matter.[4]   Nevertheless, for
us men, since we only know each other's minds through speech
and gesture, the intermediation of idea is necessary in the perception of all external objects, whether material or spiritual.[5]

We know through ideas: but what is the origin and nature
of ideas?   According to Malebranche, there are five possibilities.   His method of argumentation is to exclude four of these
hypotheses and leave the fifth standing.   And the fifth theory
is that we see all things in God.   Let us follow the argument
through.

The first hypothesis[6] is that material objects cast off species
that resemble them.   This ancient Democritean doctrine Malebranche attributes to the peripatetics.   In detail it is that these
sensible objects, being thrown off by the object, are rendered
intelligible by the "active intellect," and are then perceived by
the "passive intellect."   The foundation of this whole system
is the notion that sensible objects cast off species that resemble
them.   There are many reasons why this is an absurd hypothesis.   The first is the impenetrability of bodies.   If objects like
the sun and stars and all nearer bodies cast off species, these
species would have to be of the same nature as the bodies themselves; they would have to be gross and material.   They would
have to interpenetrate; but this is impossible.[7]   The whole of
space would be full of species; they would rub against each
other and break, and thus fail to render objects visible.   Since
from a single point we can see a great number of objects, the
species of a great many objects would necessarily concentrate
themselves to a point, which is impossible since matter is im-
penetrable.[8]   Again it is certain that the nearer an object is, the
larger it appears.   Now there is no reason why the species should
shrink.[9]   And it is still more difficult to explain on this theory
what happens to the species when one regards the object through
a magnifying glass.[9]   And so on.

The second hypothesis to fall before Malebranche's dialectic is the theory that the soul has the power to produce its own
ideas.[10]   Some maintain that our souls have the power to produce the ideas of the things of which they wish to think, and
that they are excited to produce them by the impressions that
objects make on our bodies, although these impressions are not

[4] *Recherche*, I, p. 376.
[5] *Recherche*, I, p. 375.
[6] *Recherche*, I, p. 378f.
[7] *Recherche*, I, p. 397.
[8] *Recherche*, I, p. 379.
[9] *Recherche*, I, p. 380.

supposed to be images of the objects that caused them.[10] They claim that it is in this respect that man is made in the image of God, and participates in his power; that just as God created all things from nothing and as he can annihilate them and create other things anew, thus man can create and destroy ideas of whatever things he pleases.[10] But this participation in the power of God that men boast of possessing, as it is ordinarily explained, has something of independence in it, but it is a false and chimerical independence that the vanity of men makes them imagine.[10] No one can deny that ideas are real beings and that they are capable of representing very different things. It is impossible to doubt that they are spiritual and very different from the bodies that they represent.[11] In fact, the intelligible world is more perfect than the material world, as we shall see in what follows. When we say that men have the power of forming ideas as it pleases them to form them, we run the risk of supposing that men have the power of creating beings more noble and more perfect than the world God has created.[11] Even if one were to grant the human spirit power to create and destroy the ideas of things, it could never avail itself of this power. For just as a painter, however skillful he may be in his art, cannot represent an animal he has never seen, in the same way a man cannot form the idea of an object if he does not know it beforehand, if he does not already possess the idea, and the possession of the idea does not depend on his choice.[12] But if he has the idea, it is useless to create a new idea.[12]

It is in vain that our opponents object that the mind has certain general ideas which it does not itself produce, but that it produces its particular ideas. For just as a painter cannot paint a particular man he has never seen, so the mind cannot represent to itself a horse if it only possesses ideas of being in general and animal in general.[12] It is true that when we conceive a square by pure intellection we can further imagine it. But although this cannot be explained here—we are not the cause of the existence of the image.[12] Malebranche is referring to his theory of occasional causes. Now when we do thus imagine a square on the basis of a previous intellection of it, the first idea serves as a rule for the production of the second.[13] We must not believe that images and sense-perceptions are more distinct than the ideas of pure understanding; on the contrary, the

---

[10] *Recherche*, I, p 382 It is interesting to note that Leibniz clearly perceived the dangers of this magnification of God at the expense of the creature "There is good reason," he says in one place, "also for refuting the Reverend Father Malebranche, especially when he maintains that the soul is purely passive I think I have demonstrated that every substance is active, and especially the soul" *Philosophical Works*, Duncan's Translation, p 234

[11] *Recherche*, I, p. 383.

[12] *Recherche* I p 385

[13] *Recherche*, I, p 386

ideas of sense and imagination are only distinct by reason of their conformity with the ideas of pure reason.[13]

They who hold that the mind produces its own ideas hold that the mind has the power to create with wisdom and order and yet without knowledge of what it is doing, a thing that is clearly inconceivable.[14] It is true that, ordinarily when men have desire for ideas, the ideas come; whence it is falsely concluded that the desire is the cause of the idea. As well argue that because the sun and Mars are connected at the nativity of a child who is destined to have some extraordinary thing happen, that the sun and Mars are the cause of the extraordinary event.[14] The desire is of course only the occasional cause of the manifestation of the idea.[15] The theory then that the mind creates or produces its own ideas is to be rejected.

—The third hypothesis to be submitted to criticism by Malebranche is that we see objects by means of ideas created with us.[16] But let us consider the vast number of objects of which we can have ideas. The number of geometrical figures is infinite, and if we take any particular geometrical figure, such as the ellipse, we find that there is an infinite number of species of it.[16] In the same way, we can conceive of the height of a triangle increasing to infinity, and in this way an infinite number of triangles being produced; or we can conceive of the side which serves as a base of the triangle increasing to infinity, and in this way another infinite number of triangles being produced. This general idea that the mind has of this infinite number of triangles of different species proves that, even if we cannot conceive each particular triangle of the infinity of triangles, it is because of the limitations of our minds rather than because of any essential lack of idea.[17] "If a man applied himself to the consideration of the properties of all the different species of triangles, even if he were to continue this study forever, he would never lack particular new ideas, but his mind would uselessly tire itself."[17] The mind has ideas of all things; ideas would never fail it even were it to devote centuries to the consideration of a single figure. ̄ There is an infinite number of ideas, in fact, there are as many infinite numbers of ideas as there are different figures; and since there is an infinite number of different figures the mind must have in order to know nothing but figures, an infinity of infinite number of ideas.[17]

Now is it probable that God should have created so many things with the human mind?[18] For God had at his disposal a much simpler means, as we shall see shortly.

Even were the mind a magazine of all the ideas that are

[14] *Recherche*, I, p. 387.

[15] *Recherche*, I, p. 388

[16] *Recherche*, I, p. 390

[17] *Recherche*, I, p. 391.

necessary, it would be impossible to explain how the soul should choose some of them to present to itself, how, for example, she could bring it about that she perceived at the very instant that she opened her eyes in the midst of a landscape, size, figure, distance and movement?[19] She could not even in this way perceive a single object, like the sun, when the sun is present to the eyes of the body; for it is not conceivable that she should justly divine, from among all her ideas, which one is necessary to imagine or see the sun, and to see it of such a definite size. Furthermore, it is evident that the idea or immediate object of our minds, when we think of immense spaces, of a circle in general, of an indeterminate being, is not of created nature, for created reality can be neither infinite nor general.[20]

The fourth hypothesis, which is attributed by Malebranche to his bitter opponent, Arnauld, is that the soul beholds the existence and essence of bodies in contemplating its own perfections.[21] There are persons, who hold, says Malebranche, that the soul, being made for thinking, has, in herself, that is, in considering her own perfections, all that is necessary to perceive objects; because, it is thought, being of more noble character than all the things that she distinctly conceives, she can be said to contain them all eminently, in the language of the School, that is, in a manner more lofty and noble than they are in themselves.[22] They claim that superior things include in some manner the perfections of inferior things.[22] And since they are themselves the most noble beings they know of, they flatter themselves on having in themselves in a spiritual manner whatever is in the visible world and to be able to know all that the human mind can know merely by diversely transforming themselves.[22] In a word they think that the soul is an intelligible world which contains in itself all that the material and sensible world contains and infinitely more.[22]

-    But, says Malebranche, natural vanity, love of independence and desire to resemble him who does in truth contain in himself all beings, are the causes which account for this false theory.[22] It is true that before the creation of the world, there existed only God, and that he did not produce the world without knowledge and ideas. It is true that God's ideas are not different from him himself, and that, in this manner, all creatures, even the most material and earthly, are contained in God in a spiritual and, to us, incomprehensible manner.[22] God sees all beings within himself by considering his own perfections which represent them to him. But it is not the same with created beings. They can

[18] *Recherche*, I, p 391
[19] *Recherche*, I, p 392
[20] *Recherche*, I, p. 393
[21] *Recherche*, I, p. 394
[22] *Recherche*, I, p 395

behold within themselves neither the existence nor the essence of things.[23] The human spirit can know all things, finite and infinite, but it does not contain them within itself; for the spirit can not only behold one thing and then another thing successively, but it can actually perceive the infinite even if it cannot fully comprehend it.[23] Whence it follows that not being infinite nor capable of assuming infinite modifications, it is impossible that it should behold the essence of things by considering its own perfections.[23]

We now come to the fifth and last hypothesis. That we see all things in God. It was by this theory that Malebranche was best known in his own age.

In the first place let us keep in mind that God has in himself ideas of all the beings he has created [24] Thus he beholds all these beings by considering the perfections to which they are related.[24] Furthermore, God is very intimately united with our souls; we can say that he is the place of spirits as he is the place of bodies.[24] These two things being presupposed, it follows that the mind can behold in God that which represents created beings.[25] The mind, therefore, can see in God the works of God, provided that God is willing to reveal them to it.[25] These considerations seem to prove that God would reveal the eternal ideas in his own mind rather than create an infinite number of ideas with each soul [25] It is not only very conformable to reason, but it is also apparent from the whole economy of nature, that God acts only by very simple and direct ways: that he does nothing uselessly and without reason. What distinguishes his wisdom and power is not doing small things by great means, but doing great things by small means. Thus it is that from extension alone he produces all that is admirable in nature and in the life of animals, those who believe in substantial forms, faculties, souls in animals, attribute to God a lack of intelligence in supposing that he could not create all these things from extension alone.[26] Since God could make us see whatever we see in his perfections, there is no reason to suppose that he does otherwise.[26] Nevertheless we must not conclude that because minds see all things in God in this manner that they behold his essence. Minds do not behold the divine substance as it is in itself, but solely in so far as it is relative to creatures or "participable" by them.[26] What they behold in God is very imperfect and God is very perfect We do not understand that perfect simplicity in which God includes all things.[27] Another reason for believing that we see all things in God is such that such a belief places

[23] *Recherche*, I, p. 396
[24] *Recherche*, I, p 398   Of Bouilher, p 34
[25] *Recherche*, I, p 348
[26] *Recherche*, I, p 399
[27] *Recherche* I, p 400   Rom I, 17

us in an entire dependence upon God.[27] *Non sumus sufficientes cogitare aliquid a nobis tanquam ex nobis, sed sufficientia nostra ex Deo est.*[27] He is the light of spirits and the father of light. *Pater luminum* [28] He is the light which lighteth every man that cometh into the world. *Lux vera quae, illuminat omnem hominem venientem in hunc mundum.*[29]

One of the strongest reasons for the theory of vision in God is the way in which we do, as a matter of experience, perceive things Every one knows from his experience that when we wish to think of something in particular, we first of all cast our mental look upon all beings, and we then apply ourselves to the particular object we wish to think of.[30] We can only desire to see a particular object that we do not already see on the condition that we have some vague and confused apprehension of it; thus all beings must be present to our minds, in a general and confused way, and this can only be beecause God, who contains all realities within the simplicity of his own being, is present to the mind.[30]

The mind would not be capable of having universal ideas of genera and species if it did not behold all things contained in one single being. For every creature is a particular being, and when we behold "triangle in general" we behold something which could not have been created.[31] Further, we have the idea of the infinite being, and this is in itself the most beautiful proof of God's existence. And the idea of the infinite precedes the idea of the finite; for, if we are to conceive a finite being, it is necessary to limit the idea of being in general, or the infinite.[31] The mind perceives nothing save by the idea of the infinite[31] The idea of the infinite is far from being a confused assemblage of particular ideas, on the contrary, particular ideas are "participations" of the idea of the infinite. Thus we see all things in God because God is in all things.

The ideas are effective causes, for they act on the mind, enlighten it, make it happy or miserable. Nothing can act upon the mind that is not superior in nature to it; and only God is superior in nature to the mind. Then these ideas which affect the mind must exist in the efficacious substance of the divinity.[32]

It is not possible that God should have another end for his

---

[28] *Recherche*, I, p. 400

[29] *Recherche*, I, p 401

[30] *Recherche*, I, p 401

[31] *Recherche*, I, p 402

[32] *Recherche*, I, p 403   Locke waxes facetious over this point of Malebranche's doctrine   "To conceive thus of the soul's intimate union with an infinite being, and by that union receiving of ideas, leads one as naturally into gross thoughts, as a country maid would have of an infinite butter-print, in which were engraven figures of all sorts and sizes, the several parts whereof being, as there was occasion, applied to her lump of butter, left on it the figure or idea there was present need of" *Examination of P Malebranche's Opinion of Seeing All Things in God* Locke's *Philosophical Works*, Bohn Library, Vol II, p 413 The quotation is from p 425

actions than himself. It is therefore necessary that not only does our natural love tend towards him, but that the knowledge and light he gives us let us know something that is within him. Otherwise what comes from God would not be for his sake. If God had created a mind and given it as an idea the sun, then God would have made that mind and that idea, not for his own sake, but for the sake of the sun.[33] God cannot make a mind able to behold his works if that mind does not behold God in beholding his works. Thus we can say that if we did not see God, we should see nothing, just as, if we did not love God, we should love nothing.[34]

But when it is said that we see sensible and material things in God, we must guard against the notion that we have our feeling in God.[35] God is active within us, and he *knows* sensible things, but he does not feel them. We must distinguish between *sentiment* and *idée pure*. The first is a modification of our souls and God is the cause of it, but he causes it without feeling this *sentiment*. On the other hand, the idea that accompanies the feeling is in God, and we see it there because it pleases God to reveal it to us.[36] God joins the sensation to the idea when the objects are present to us that we may be aware of them and enter into the sentiments and passions we ought to have in relation to them.[36]

Spirits behold the eternal truths in God by reason of their essential union with the word, or divine wisdom.[36] On the other hand, they perceive the moral and imperative laws by reason of the perpetual impression that they receive from the will of God, which bears them towards him, and tries, so to speak, to make their wills entirely like his. In this way they know that the eternal order is their indispensable law; an order which includes within itself all the eternal laws, such as that we ought to love the good and flee from the evil, love justice more than riches, obey God rather than men and an infinity of other natural laws.[36] It is by this dependence upon God, by the union of our mind with the Word, or divine wisdom, and of our wills with the divine love, that we are made in the image and resemblance of God.[36] This resemblance has been effaced by sin, but if we bear the image of the Word humiliated on earth and follow the movements of the Holy Spirit, the original union of our minds with the Word of the Father, and the love of the Father and the Son will be re-established.[37]

These, then, are reasons which lead one to believe that minds perceive all things by the intimate presence of him who compre-

[33] *Recherche*, I, p. 403.
[34] *Recherche*, I, p. 404.
[35] *Recherche*. I, p. 406.
[36] *Recherche*, I, p. 407.
[37] *Recherche*, I, p. 408.

hends all things in the simplicity of his being [38] God is the intelligible world, the place of spirits, just as the material world is the place of bodies. From his power, spirits receive all their modifications; in his wisdom, they find all their ideas, and it is by his love that they are moved in all their lawful movements. *Non longe est ab unoquoque nostrum, in ipso enim vivimus, movemur et sumus.*[39]

Malebranche's epistemology is completed in the four-fold division of knowledge which we find in the *Recherche*, Book III, Part II, Chapter VII.

The first kind of knowledge is knowledge of things by themselves. God alone is known in this way. It is God alone that we behold by a direct and immediate vision, in which that which is known illumines the spirit by its own substance.[40] No finite being can represent the infinite, being without restriction, universal being.[40] On the other hand it is not difficult to conceive that finite beings can be represented by the infinite being that includes them in its *"substance très-efficace."* We thus know God by himself, although, to be sure, in a very imperfect manner[41]

The second kind of knowledge is through ideas, that is, through something different from the things known themselves. Everything in the world of which we have any sort of knowledge is either mind or matter. We know bodies and their properties only through ideas. It is in God and by means of their ideas, and for this reason the knowledge that we have of them is very perfect; the idea of extension is enough to inform us of all the properties extension can have, and we cannot desire to have an idea more distinct and more fruitful than that of extension.[41]

It is not the same with souls, and here we come upon the third kind of knowledge. We do not behold the idea of the soul

[38] Cf Ollé-Laprune, *La philosophie de Malebranche*, Vol I, p. 238f, and Kuno Fischer, *Geschichte der neuern Philosophie*, Vol II, Ed 5, p 68. We may observe that Leibniz virtually accepts the doctrine of Vision in God "It is also true," says Leibniz, "that in God is the source not only of existences but also of essences, so far as they are real, of that which is real in the possible This is because the understanding of God is the region of eternal truths, or of the ideas on which they depend, and because without him, there would be nothing real in the possibilities, and not only nothing existing, but also nothing possible" *Monadology*, No 43 *Philosophical Works*, Tr Duncan, p 224 Speaking directly of Malebranche's Vision in God, he says· "I say that it is an expression which may be excused and even praised, provided it be rightly taken, . It is, therefore, well to observe that not only in Malebranche's system but also in mine, God alone is the immediate external object of souls, exercising upon them a real influence And although the current school seems to admit other influences by means of certain species, which it believes that objects convey into the soul, it does not fail to recognize that all our perfections are a continual gift of God, and a limited participation in his infinite perfection. This suffices to show that what is true and good in our knowledge is still an emanation from the light of God, and that it is in this sense that it may be said that *we see all things in God*" *Op cit.*, p 237

[39] *Recherche*, I, p 409 Cf Joly, p 64ff and 70ff

[40] *Recherche*, I, p. 411.

[41] *Recherche*, I, p 412

in God.[42] We only know the soul by *conscience*, and it is for this reason that our knowledge is imperfect.[42] If we beheld in God the idea that corresponds to our soul, we should know all the properties of which it is capable, just as we know all the properties of which extension is capable by contemplation of the eternal idea of extension.[42]

The fourth kind of knowledge Malebranche calls knowledge by conjecture. This is the knowledge that we have of the souls of other men and of pure intelligences. We have no direct knowledge of them either in themselves or by their ideas, and as they are different from us it is not possible that we know them by *conscience*.[43] We "conjecture" that the souls of other men are of the same species with our own. What we feel we suppose that they feel, and even where these feelings are not related to the body, we are sure that we are not deceived because we see in God certain ideas and immutable laws according to which, as we are certain, God acts on all spirits.[43]

Malebranche and St. Augustine.

The origin of the doctrine of Vision in God is undoubtedly to be found in the writings of St. Augustine. From this point of view Malebranche's discussion in the Preface to the *Recherche* is important. – St. Augustine, says Malebranche, speaks in a thousand places in his works of the intimate union of God and man, and of this union as the life, light, and felicity of the soul.[44] Malebranche is astonished that Christian philosophers should be content to regard the soul as merely the *form* of the body, and to neglect its union with God. - In truth, in proportion as a soul is united with God it becomes purer, more luminous, stronger and of broader extent. On the other hand, the union of the soul with the body is the measure of the corruption, weakness and blindness of the soul.[45] As St. Augustine says, "Eternal wisdom is the principle of all creatures capable of intelligence, and this wisdom, which remains always the same, never ceases to speak to its creatures in the secret depths of their minds, that they may turn towards their principle; for it is only the vision of eternal wisdom which gives being to minds, which completes them and gives them the last perfection of which they are capable." (*Principium creaturae intellectualis est aeterna sapientia, quod principium manens in se incommutabiliter nullo modo cessat occulta inspiratione vocationis loqui ei creaturae cui principium est, ut convertatur ad id est quo est; quod aliter formata*

---

[42] *Recherche*, I, p. 413.

[43] *Recherche*, p. 416. On the four kinds of knowledge, cf. Kuno Fischer, *Geschichte derneuern Philosophie*, Vol. II, Ed. 5, p. 66.

[44] *Recherche*, I, p. i.

[45] *Recherche*, I, p. viii.

ac perfecta non possit. De Genesi ad litteram. Ch 50)[46] –This mighty doctrine of Augustine is indeed the basis of the whole system of Malebranche. God is our only master and can alone instruct us, and this he does by the manifestation of his substance.– As Augustine says: *"Insinuavit nobis (Christus) animam humanum et mentem rationalem non vegetari, non illuminari, non beatificari nisi ipsa substantia Dei."*[47]

Human teachers are, as Augustine again says, only *monitors.* They are neither masters nor teachers. They do not speak with their own authority but are only representatives of eternal wisdom.[48] We are not our own lights but we draw all our light from God: *Noli putare te ipsum esse lucam.*[49] *Non a me mihi lumen existens, sed lumen non participas nisi in TE.*[50]

Malebranche and Locke.

At this point we may note certain criticisms and comments upon the doctrine of Malebranche. In the first place, an interesting commentary on the philosophy of Malebranche, or, more particularly, on his epistemology, is Locke's *"Examination of P. Malebranche's Opinion of Seeing All Things in God "*[51] It is, of course, written from the general standpoint for which Locke is so well known. He refers to Malebranche as "acute and ingenious," and as having a "great many very fine thoughts, judicious reasonings, and uncommon reflections."[52] Malebranche's proof by elimination of the theory of the Vision in God is at fault; it "loses all its force as soon as we consider the weakness of our minds and the narrowness of our capacities, and have but humility enough to allow that there may be many things which we cannot fully comprehend, and that God is not bound in all he does to subject his ways of operation to the scrutiny of our thoughts, and confine himself to do nothing but what we must comprehend."[53] The most significant point, however, is that Locke clearly perceives that Malebranche's philosophy leads to subjective idealism. "He further says," continues Locke, "that had we a magazine of all ideas that are necessary for seeing things, they would be of no use, since the mind could not know which to choose, and set before itself to see the sun What

[46] *Recherche,* I, p ix

[47] *Recherche,* I, p xi   Malebranche gives the reference to Augustine, *In Joan Tr* 23

[48] Malebranche here refers us to Augustine, *De Magistro,* XVII

[49] Malebranche's reference is, *In Psal.,* XVII

[50] The reference is *De Verbis Domini,* Ser 8   Cf *Saint Augustine,* J Martin, Paris, 1907, for a very scholarly account of the teachings of St Augustine   Cf also *The Doctrine of the Self in St Augustine and in Descartes,* Marguerite Witmer Kehr, Philosophical Review, XXV

[51] *Philosophical Works,* Bohn Library, Vol II p 413.

[52] *Op cit,* p 414.

[53] *Idem*

he here means by the sun is hard to conceive; and, according to
this hypothesis of Seeing All Things in God, how can he know
that there is any such real being as the sun? Did he ever see
the sun? No, but on occasion the presence of the sun to his
eyes, he has the idea of the sun in God, which God has exhibited
to him; but the sun, because it cannot be united to his soul, he
cannot see. How then does he know that there is a sun which
he never saw? And since God does all things by the most com-
pendious ways, what need is there that God should make a sun
that we might see its idea in him when he pleased to exhibit it,
when this might as well be done without any real sun at all.''[54]
Locke does not seem to have suspected that his own theory of
knowledge could be developed in the same direction.˙ '' 'Perhaps
it is God alone,' says our author,'' writes Locke, '' 'who can en-
ligten our mind by his substance' When I know what the *substance* of God is, and what it is to be *enlightened by that substance,* I shall know what I also shall think of it, but at present
I confess myself in the dark as to this matter, nor do these good
words of *substance* and *enlightening,* in the way they are here
used, help me one jot out of it.''[55] On the whole, however, it
must be said that Locke's habits of thought were so opposed to
those of Malebranche that he seldom gets beyond a superficial
understanding of him.[56]

Malebranche and Berkeley.

Berkeley's reaction to Malebranche sets the difference of
their systems in a clear light In the Second Dialogue between
Hylas and Philonous the famous English philosopher considers
the doctrine of Vision in God as compared with his own theory.
Hylas asks, concerning Berkeley's idealism, ''Do you not think˙
it looks very like a notion entertained by some eminent moderns,
of *Seeing All Things in God?*''[57] But Philonous cannot understand how ideas which are things all together passive and inert,
can be the essence, or any part (or like any part) of the essence
of God, who is an impassive, indivisible, pure, active being. ''It
makes the material world serve to no purpose ''[58] The difference between Malebranche's rationalism and Berkeley's empiricism comes clearly to light when Philonous says of Malebranche,
''He builds on the most general abstract ideas, which I entirely
disclaim.''[59] ''It must be owned that I entirely agree with what

---

[54] *Op cit*, p. 425

[55] *Op cit*, p 444

[56] On this point *cf* Ollion. *La philosophie générale de John Locke,* p 402 And
for a discussion of Locke's criticism of Malebranche, *cf* Ollé-Laprune, *La philosophie
de Malebranche,* Vol II, p. 33f.

[57] *Works,* Ed Fraser. Vol I, p 305

[58] *Op cit,* p 306

[59] *Idem*

the Holy Scripture saith, 'That in God we live and move and
have our being.'' But that we see things in his essence, after the
manner above set forth, I am far from believing. Take here in
brief my meaning—it is evident that the things I perceive are
my own ideas, and that no idea can exist unless it be in a mind.
Nor it is less plain that these ideas or things by me perceived,
either themselves or their archetypes, exist independently of my
mind; since I know myself not to be their author, it being out
of my power to determine at pleasure what particular ideas I
shall be affected with upon opening my eyes or ears.''[60] These
"things" or "ideas" or "sensations" must then exist in some
other mind. Whence Philonous concludes, *"there is a Mind
which affects me every moment with all the sensible impressions
I perceive.* And, from the variety, order, and manner of these,
I conclude the Author of them to be wise, powerful and good
beyond comprehension. Mark it well; I do not say, I see things
by perceiving that which represents them in the intelligible Substance of God. This I do not understand, but I say, the things
by me perceived are known by the understanding, and are produced by the will of an infinite Spirit.''[61] The difference between Malebranche and Berkeley is, of course, more important
than any superficial resemblance between their systems. In the
former the criterion of reality is, ultimately, logical intelligibil-
ity, *i. e.*, the possibility of being *clearly conceived,* while for the
latter the standard of reality is—with certain well-known exceptions—the possibility of being reduced to the experience of the
senses. On the one side, the Idea of Plato; on the other, what
Hume calls an impression, is taken as the crucial instance of
reality

Malebranche and Arnauld.

Perhaps the most interesting comment on Malebranche's
epistemology, from certain points of view, is that contained in
the criticism which Arnauld brought against Malebranche's theory of ideas.[62]. Certain passages in Malebranche's writings
suggest what is called in contemporary philosophy, "Representative Perceptionism," and he was attacked on that score by
Arnauld These passages, however, do not seem to represent the
true spirit of his teaching. Although in the above cited passages he speaks of ideas representing bodies to us, his deeper
meaning was always that ideas represent objects in God, not by
copying them, but by expressing their real significance. We
know objects through ideas, not as we know the original of a

[60] *Op cit.,* p 307

[61] *Op cit.,* p 308

[62] For a fairly detailed account of Arnauld's criticism of Malebranche, see M
Ginsberg, *The Nature of Knowledge as conceived by Malebranche.* Proceedings of the
Aristotelian Society, 1916-17, pp 182-194

painting through the picture, but as we know the instance through the law, the fact through the theory, the act through the will which it expresses. The great Jansenist theologian was bent on overturning Malebranche's system in every detail, and he therefore centered his attack upon what seemed its pivotal point, the doctrine of ideas. Taking his stand upon certain passages in Malebranche's writings, which do not seem to express the real spirit of the latter's teaching, he regarded Malebranche's ideas as *êtres representatifs*, representative beings, entities distinct from the act or modality of the soul by which it knows, on the one hand, and from the object known, on the other. He thus accuses Malebranche of representative perceptionism. His own position is that it is the nature of the soul to think of, and to know, objects external to itself, and that there is no need for the intermediation of ideas between the soul and its object. That which exists *formally* in nature, is capable of existing *objectively* in the mind. This capacity which the soul possesses of having objects present to it *objectively* constitutes its very essence and needs no explanation. If the term idea is to be used it must stand merely for the soul's act of perception. The notion of ideas as representative entities interposed between the soul and its object is based upon a crude analogy between intellectual and bodily vision. In the latter case, the object seen must be either *present* itself, or be *represented by some image*, as when we see things in mirrors. These things do not hold of intellectual vision and the whole notion of "ideas" is simply a fiction.

Arnauld thus foreshadows Reid in his attack upon the "way of ideas." "When we say," says Arnauld, "that our ideas and our perceptions (for I take these for the same thing) represent to us the things which we conceive, and are images of them, it is in an entirely different sense than when we say that pictures represent their originals, or that spoken or written words are images of our thoughts; for with regard to ideas it means that the things which we conceive are *objectively* in our mind and in our thoughts. Now this *way of being objectively in the mind*, is so peculiar to mind and thought, as being that which makes up its peculiar nature, that we seek in vain for anything similar in all that is not mind and thought. And, as I have remarked, what has confused this whole matter of *ideas*, is that one has desired to explain, by comparisons taken from corporeal things, the manner in which objects are represented by our ideas, although there can be no true comparison between body and mind.[63] On the basis of considerations of this sort, Arnauld completely denies the existence of ideas as representative entities. With this denial he believes himself to have overthrown the

---

[63] *Des vraies et des fausses idées, Oeuvres Philosophiques de Antoine Arnauld*, edited by Jules Simon, 1843, p 52

very foundations of Malebranche's system. As a matter of fact,
it is easy to see that his arguments were really beside the point
For the divine ideas through which we contemplate things were
not essentially representative entities. They were not copies of
things, but representatives of things. We owe to Arnauld's
attack, however, a very clear re-statement on the part of Malebranche of his position. "A serious reflection," he says in his
first reply, "upon the difference which is to be found between
knowing by *feeling* (sentiment) and knowing by *idea,* or rather
between *knowing* and *feeling,* between *knowing* numbers and
their properties, extension, geometrical figures and their relations, and *feeling* pleasure, pain, heat, color, and even the inner
perceptions which we have of objects, gives reason enough, it
seems to me, for those who are accustomed to metaphysical spec-
ulation to conclude

I That to *feel pain,* for example it is not necessary to have
a representative *idea,* and that the modality of the soul is sufficient; because it is certain that pain is a modality or modification of the soul;

II. That to know numbers and geometrical figures and relations one needs an *idea,* in order that the soul can have perception of them; for without *idea,* the soul has perception of
nothing distinguished from itself, and the *idea of a circle* cannot be a *modality* of the soul;

III. That in order to see a sensible object, the sun, a tree,
a house, *etc.,* two things are needed, the *modality of color,* for
M. Arnauld agrees that color is a modification of the soul, and a
pure idea, namely the idea of extension, or intelligible extension; for when one has a lively sensation of light, attached to a
distant intelligible circle in a certain intelligible space, rendered
sensible by certain colors, one sees the sun, not as it is, but as one
sees it (*sic*). Here, Sir, is all that is necessary to *feel* that which
passes in the soul, *to learn sciences,* and to *see* all the objects of
this visible world."[64] This passage shows that Malebranche regarded the idea as the *essence* of the sensible thing, as its *meaning* or *nature,* without which it could not exist, not as a copy or
picture of it. For these reasons Arnauld's attack can be regarded as largely irrelevant, although it had a certain justifica-
tion in the looseness of terminology with which Malebranche
expressed himself.[65]

[64] *Idem.*
[65] *Of* the interesting discussion in Olle Laprune, *La Philosophie de Malebranche,*
Vol II, p 7ff

CHAPTER V: MALEBRANCHE'S METHODOLOGY.

We are now in a position to examine Malebranche's contribution to methodology.[1] The Sixth Book of the *Recherche* is a complete exposition of the rationalistic ideal of scientific and philosophical method. We shall see here how true Malebranche was to the spirit of Descartes, and especially to the Descartes of the *Regulae ad directionem ingenii,* as Cassirer points out.[2] First of all, we may note that Malebranche divides his discussion into two parts: the first treats of means for rendering the mind attentive; the second, of the rules to be followed in the search for truth.[3]

Aids to Attention.

Understanding has the exclusive function of perceiving; there is no difference, as far as understanding is concerned, between simple perceptions, judgments and reasonings.[4] Judgments and reasonings, however, are much more complex than simple perceptions, because they not only represent several things to the mind, but also relations between several things.[4] Simple perceptions only present *things* to the mind; judgments present relations between things, and reasonings relations between relations.[4] Nevertheless simple perception, judgment and reasoning are only three levels of complexity in the same process.[4] And since judgment and reasoning are only complex perceptions (as far as understanding is concerned) error is inconceivable; for we cannot conceive how a pure perception should be in error.[5] One can see that 2 times 2 equals 4 and that 2 times 2 is not 5, for there really is a relation of equality between 2 times 2 and 4 and of inequality between 2 times 2 and 5; thus the perception of truth is intelligible.[5] But no one will ever see that 2 times 2 is 5. Error then consists solely in a precipitous consent of the will which permits itself to be dazzled by some false gleam, and in the place of preserving its liberty as much as possible rests negligently in the appearance of truth.[6]

We must seek means then that will prevent our perceptions from being confused and imperfect. And as there is nothing that renders perceptions more clear and distinct than attention we must attempt to discover methods of becoming more atten-

---

[1] For an interesting constructive interpretation of Malebranche's methodology, *cf.* Novaro, *Die Philosophie des Nicolaus Malebranche,* p. 7f.

[2] *Erkenntnisproblem,* I, p. 563.

[3] *Recherche,* II, p. 261.

[4] *Recherche,* II, p. 262.

[5] *Recherche,* II, p. 263

tive than we are. In this way we must *"conserver l'evidence"* in our reasonings, and see in a single view a necessary connection between the parts of the longest deductions.[5] Now the mind naturally applies itself not to abstract ideas but to sensible things.[6] Hence all who would seriously devote themselves to the pursuit of truth ought to avoid all strong sensations, such as loud noises, too bright light, pleasure and pain. They ought to guard ceaselessly the purity of their imaginations lest there be traced in their brains too deep vestiges which would continually disturb and dissipate the mind [6] They ought to prevent every movement of the passions. Although the pure ideas of truth are always present to us, we cannot contemplate them when the mind is occupied with these disturbing modifications.[6]

Nevertheless there is a positive side to passion and sense. There are useful passions which give us the force and courage to overcome the pain that is involved in attention.[7] Good passions are the desire to discover the truth, to acquire sufficient light to conduct oneself, to render oneself useful to one's neighbor. Bad passions are desire to acquire a reputation, to establish oneself, to rise above one's equal and other still more lawless passions.[7] The passion for glory can be related to a good end, and it is permitted to some persons and on certain occasions to avail themselves of this passion to render themselves more attentive.[8] But it is indeed necessary to take care in making use of this passion, which is liable to lead us insensibly into bad studies which have more glitter than utility or truth.[8]

Malebranche was deeply convinced of the philosophical value of mathematical studies. He regards geometry as a species of universal science which opens the mind, renders it attentive, and gives it skill in controlling the imagination. One can compare this conviction with that of Plato, who, in the *Republic*, says: "That the knowledge at which geometry aims is knowledge of the eternal, and not of aught perishing and transient. . . . Geometry will draw the soul towards truth and create the spirit of philosophy and raise up that which is now unhappily allowed to fall down.'"[9]

In Book VI, Chapter V, of the *Recherche*, Malebranche pursues the same theme with respect to arithmetic and algebra. Of all the sciences, says Malebranche, arithmetic and geometry are the principal ones that teach us to think with "skill and light and admirable management of the mind.'"[10] Ordinarily geometry does not perfect the intellect so much as the imagination and the truths discovered by this science are not always as evi-

[5] *Recherche*, II, p 266
[7] *Recherche*, II, p 267
[8] *Recherche*, II, p 268
[9] Jowett's Translation. Book VII.
[10] *Recherche*, II, p 302

dent as geometricians imagine.[11] Arithmetic, with its basic idea[11] [30]
of equality, is a more enlightening science.[11] And algebra is
still more important than arithmetic; it divides the power of
the mind still less, and abbreviates ideas in the simplest and
easiest manner that can be conceived.[12] What can only be done
in arithmetic in a great deal of time, can be done in a moment
in algebra.[12] These two sciences are the foundations of all the
rest and give us the true means for mastering all the exact sciences; one cannot utilize to a greater advantage the capacity of
the mind than in arithmetic and algebra.

The Rules of Method.

The preceding methodological discussion may be regarded
as concerned, in general, with means of availing oneself of the
power of attention, of concentrating and focusing the mind. In
the Second Part of the Sixth Book, *De la Méthode,* of the *Recherche,* Malebranche discusses certain rules that are to be followed in the pursuit of truth. The principle of all the rules is
that in order to discover the truth without fear of deception it
is always necessary *"conserver l'evidence dans ses raisonne-
ment,"* that is, our reasonings must always be clear and com-
pelling.[13] This may be compared with the first of Descartes'
four rules of method, which is stated in the *Discourse on Method*
as follows: "To accept nothing as true which I did not clearly
recognize to be so."[14] From this we may derive a rule in regard
to the subject matter of our studies. we should reason only concerning things of which we can have clear ideas.[15] As Descartes
says in his *Regulae*: "Only those objects should engage our attention to the sure and indubitable knowledge of which our mental powers seem to be adequate."[16] Hence we should always
commence with the easiest and simplest things and remain with
them a long time before undertaking the investigation of the
more complex and difficult [17] As Descartes says: "We ought
to give the whole of our attention to the most insignificant and
most easily mastered facts, and remain a long time in the contemplation of them until we are accustomed to behold the truth
clearly and distinctly."[18]

As for rules governing the procedure of our thought, as
distinct from rules governing the choice of the subject-matter,
Malebranche proposes the following: First, we must conceive
very clearly the question which we are attempting to answer.
This rule corresponds to Descartes' Rule XIII, which runs:

[11] *Recherche,* II, p 302ff
[12] *Recherche,* II, p 306
[13] *Recherche,* II, p 308
[14] *Philosophical Works;* Tr Ross and Haldane, Vol I, p 92
[15] *Recherche,* II, p 308
[16] *Op. cit ,* Vol I, p 3, Rule II
[17] *Recherche,* II, p 308.
[18] *Op cit ,* Vol I, p 28, Rule IX

"Once a 'question' is perfectly understood, we must free it of every conception superfluous to its meaning, state it in its simplest terms, and, having recourse to an enumeration, split it up into the various sections beyond which analysis cannot go in minuteness."[19]

As a second rule, Malebranche has: We must discover by an effort of mind one or more intermediate ideas which can serve as a common nature in the discovery of relations.[20] To this may be compared Descartes': "If we wish our science to be complete, those matters which promote the end we have in view must one and all be scrutinized by a movement of thought which is continuous and nowhere interrupted; they must also be included in an enumeration which is both adequate and methodical."[21] Thirdly, says Malebranche, we must eliminate from the subject under investigation all things that are not necessary for the discovery of the particular truth we seek This may be compared with the rule from Descartes we have just correlated with Malebranche's first rule. In the fourth place, says Malebranche, we must divide the subject of meditation into parts, and consider them all, one after another in their natural order, beginning with the simplest, that is, with those that involve fewest relations, and never passing to the more complex save when we have clearly grasped the simpler, and rendered them familiar.[22] With this we may compare Descartes' Rule V: "Method consists entirely in the order and disposition of the objects toward which our mental vision must be directed if we would find out any truth. We shall comply with it exactly if we reduce involved and obscure propositions step by step to those that are simpler and then starting with the intuitive apprehension of all those that are absolutely simple attempt to ascend to the knowledge of all others by precisely similar steps [23] In the fifth place, says Malebranche, we should abbreviate our ideas and then arrange them in our imagination, or write them down on paper, so that they may not occupy too much of the capacity of the mind.[24] Now to this we may compare Descartes' Rule XVI, "When we come across matters which do not require our present attention, it is better, even though they are necessary to our conclusion, to represent them by highly abbreviated symbols, rather than by complete figures This guards against error due to defective memory, on the one hand, and, on the other, prevents that distraction of thought which an effort to keep those matters in mind while attending to other instances

[19] *Op cit*, Vol I, p 49
[20] *Recherche*, II, p 309
[21] *Op cit*, Vol I, p 19 Rule VII.
[22] *Recherche* II, p 309
[23] *Op. c t.*, p 14
[24] *Recherche*, II, p 309

would cause.'[25] In the sixth place, we should compare all our ideas according to the rules of combination, says Malebranche, either alternately one with another, or by a single glance of the mind, or by a movement of the imagination accompanied by a glance of the intellect or by the calculation of the pen joined with attention of mind and imagination.[26] And in correspondence with this we have Descartes' Rule IX, "If, after we have recognized intuitively a number of simple truths, we wish to draw any inference from them, it is useful to run them over in a continuous and uninterrupted act of thought, to reflect upon their relations to one another, and to grasp together distinctly' a number of these propositions as far as is possible at the same time. For this is a way of making our knowledge much more certain and of greatly increasing the power of the mind.[27]

We must guard against contenting ourselves with some gleam of probability and repeat the comparisons so often that we cannot avoid believing without feeling the secret reproaches of the Master, Eternal Reason[28] The necessary rules are not many in number; and they all mutually depend upon each other.[28] They are natural and can be made so familiar that it is not necessary to think of them much of the time that one is using them.[28] They are capable of governing the attention of the mind without dividing it.[28] But in order to understand the importance of these rules it is necessary to see the errors into which philosophers fall who do not apply them.

The philosophers of the School do not follow the first and most elementary rule of exact thought which is to reason only concerning that of which we have clear ideas, and to commence with what is simple and advance to what is complex.[29] Aristotle, who well merits the title of the prince of these philosophers, in Malebranche's opinion, almost always reasons according to confused ideas received by sense and on certain other vague and indeterminate ideas which represent nothing in particular to the mind[29] Aristotle's physics is the worst example of this.[30] At the basis of it all is the notion that the sensible qualities of things belong to the things themselves rather than to our minds.[31] If one asks for example those who have passed their entire lives in the reading of the ancient philosophers and physicians (*médecins*) as to whether water is humid, fire dry, wine hot, the blood of fishes cold, or as to whether plants and animals have souls, they will reply at once without consulting

[25] *Op cit*, p 66
[26] *Recherche*, II, p 310
[27] *Op cit*, p 33 For a comparison of the methods of Descartes and Malebranche along more general lines *cf* Ollé Laprune, *La philosophie de Malebranche*, Vol I, p 79ff
[28] *Recherche*, II p 311
[29] *Recherche*, II, p 312
[30] *Recherche*, II, p 313
[31] *Recherche* II, p. 314

anything but their sense and their memory of what they have read. They do not see that these terms are all equivocal, and they find it strange that one should care to define them. They grow impatient if one tries to make them see that they are going too fast and that their senses are misleading them.[32] If we remember that the greater part of the questions of philosophers and physicians include such equivocal terms as we have just mentioned, we cannot avoid believing that there is nothing solid in all of their big books.[33] Descartes proceeded in another way; he knew how to distinguish things from each other and he did not answer questions with ideas drawn from sense-impression. If people would take the trouble to read him, they would find that he explains in a clear and evident manner the chief effects of nature solely from the ideas of extension, figure, and movement [33]

Besides ideas drawn from sense-perception, the philosophers of the School use general logical terms by means of which they can explain anything without having any special knkowledge of it.[33] Such terms are *genus, species, act, power, nature, form, faculty, quality, cause in itself*, and *cause by accident*, etc [33] The partisans of Aristotle do not understand that these words signify nothing and that one is no wiser after one knows that fire dissolves metals because it has the faculty of dissolving, and that a man does not digest because he has a weak stomach or because his *faculté concoctrice* does not perform its functions well.[33] Senna purges because of its purgative quality, bread nourishes because of its nutritive quality, these propositions are not erroneous, but they have no significance. They do not involve us in error, but they are entirely useless in the pursuit of truth.

The most dangerous fallacy in the philosophy of the ancients, which arose because the ancients did not follow the maxims of the method of clear ideas, was the notion that there are certain subordinate powers in nature If we consider attentively the idea of cause or power of action we see that this idea contains something divine in it.[34] The idea of a sovereign power is the idea of a sovereign divinity, and the idea of a subordinate power is the idea of an inferior divinity.[34] We therefore admit that there is something divine in the bodies that surround us if we admit that there are forms, faculties, virtues, or real beings or any other beings capable of producing effects by the force of their own nature.[35] We necessarily tend to adopt the feelings of the pagans if we respect their philosophy.[35] It is hard to persuade oneself that one should neither love nor fear real powers that act upon us;[35] and love and fear being genuine adora-

[32] *Recherche*, II, p 317
[33] *Recherche*, II, p 318
[34] *Recherche*, II, p. 322
[35] *Recherche*, II, p. 323.

tion, we can hardly avoid adoring what we love and fear [36] Thus the admission of subordinate powers into nature is the basis of pagan polytheism. But the development of this theme, which leads into Malebranche's whole scheme of occasional causes, may well be postponed to a later chapter.

The rule that we should begin with the simple and advance to the complex was completely disregarded by the scholastics. This rule is contrary to the natural inclination of men, who naturally despise the simple because it appears too easy.[37] The mind has a natural striving for the infinite and love of what is obscure and mysterious.[37] The reason is, not that the mind really loves shadows, but that it hopes to find in the shadows the good that it desires, and which it knows cannot be attained in broad daylight in this world.[37] Vanity also leads minds to plunge into the great and extraordinary.[38] Experience teaches that exact knowledge of ordinary things gives no reputation in the world, and determines those who are more sensitive to vanity than to truth to search blindly for a specious knowledge of all that is grandiose, rare and obscure.[38] Many reject the philosophy of Descartes for the amusing reason that its principles are too simple and easy.[38] There are no obscure and mysterious terms in his philosophy; women and people who know neither Greek nor Latin can understand it, therefore it is thought worthless. It is imagined that principles so simple and clear cannot explain nature and that it is better to use incomprehensible principles of explanation.[38]

The Fourth Chapter of the Sixth Book, Part II, of the *Recherche* elucidates this point at length, but along lines with which we are now familiar. It also develops in some detail Descartes' vortex theory of the universe. Time prevents any consideration of this latter development. The Fifth Chapter is an intensive critique of the peripatetic system and in particular of Aristotle's *De Coelo*. The Sixth Chapter, "General Advice Necessary to Conduct One's Investigation of Truth," etc., adds little or nothing to what has already been said. The Seventh Chapter, "On the Use of the First Rule as Regards Particular Questions," and the Eighth Chapter, "Application of the Rules to Particular Questions," while valuable and suggestive in themselves, call for no particular comment here. The same is true of the Ninth Chapter, which deals with the cause of hardness, that is, of the union of the parts of bodies with each other, from the standpoint of method.

Malebranche's philosophical ideal now stands before us In spirit it is identical with the spirit of exact science, which has always found its philosophical foundation in rationalistic phil-

[36] *Recherche*, II, p 324
[37] *Recherche*, II, p. 336
[38] *Recherche*, II, p 337.

osophy, or rather in philosophy that is deep enough to be both rationalistic and empiristic. As Novaro says: "In general, as has been said, he (Malebranche) does not combat sense and experience as such, but rather unscientific empiricism and that empty scholastic philosophy which bases natural science upon particular facts of sense and arbitrary conceptions, that same philosophy which Galileo fought in his *Dialogues*. Malebranche opposes reason or science, that is, scientific experience, to mere empirical knowledge and regards this latter as the first stage of knowledge in which man is the center and measure of all things, and draws no distinction between their subjective and objective aspects.[39]

39 *Philosophie des N Malebranche*, p 13   *Cf* Bouillier, 108f.

CHAPTER VI: MALEBRANCHE'S METAPHYSICS AND THEOLOGY.

Schopenhauer, in the Preface to the *World as Will and Idea,* remarks of his own system: "A single thought, however comprehensive it may be, must preserve the most perfect unity. If it admits of being broken up into parts to facilitate its communication the connection of these parts must yet be organic, *i. e.,* it must be a connection in which every part supports the whole just as much as it is supported by it, a connection in which there is no first and last, in which the whole thought gains distinctness through every part, and even the smallest part cannot be completely understood unless the whole has already been grasped. A book, however, must always have a first and last line, and in this respect will always remain very unlike an organism, however like one its content may be; thus form and matter are here in contradiction."[1] The same is true, of course, of any philosophical system and is particularly true of so closely integrated a system as that of Malebranche. It has frequently been necessary in our expositions of the Psychology, Epistemology and Methodology of Malebranche to assume conceptions which cannot be understood save in the light of his metaphysical doctrine. It is now to this central doctrine that we turn our attention. Here our guide is the *Entretiens sur la métaphysique et la religion,* which, as Joly says, is *"l'oeuvre ou il faut chercher le fruit le plus substantiel de sa pleine maturité."*[2] Here Malebranche's system is expounded in systematic and complete form, and the center of gravity is no longer, as in the *Recherche,* in psychology and theory of knowledge, but is rather in metaphysics and theology.

Mind and Body.

The *Premier Entretien* establishes the distinction between mind and body. Indeed, as Kuno Fischer says:—"The fundamental speculative question, which dominates the doctrine of our philosopher (Malebranche), lies in the application of dualistic principles to the possibility of our knowledge of things:—How can the essence of bodies become known to the mind, if there is between mind and body no natural community but on the contrary a complete opposition?"[3] —

The discussion opens with the proposition that *the Nothing has no properties.*[4] From this Malebranche advances to the Car-

[1] *World as Will and Idea,* Trans. Haldane and Kemp, Vol. I, p. viii
[2] *Joly,* p. 55.
[3] *Geschichte der neuern Philosophie,* Vol. II, Ed. 5, p. 54.
[4] *Entretiens,* p. 5. *Cf.* Novaro, *op. cit.,* p. 26.

tesian *cogito, ergo sum.* I think, hence I am. But what am I, I who think, at the time that I think? Am I body, spirit, man? In the first place, I know nothing of that; I only know that when I think I am something which thinks But can a body think? Can something which is extended in length, breadth, and depth, reason, desire, or feel? Beyond a doubt, no; for all the ways of existing (*maniéres d'etre*) of such an extended thing consist solely of relations of distance; and it is evident that these relations are not perceptions, reasonings, pleasures, desires, or feelings, not, in a word, thoughts. Hence this "I" that thinks is not a body.[5]

⎯ The essence of mind then is pure thought as Descartes has said.[6] And it is clear that thought as pure thought is eternally distinct from matter as pure extension. But perhaps matter is something besides extension. Perhaps my body is something besides extension, for it seems that it is my finger that feels the pain of a wound, my heart that desires, my brain that reasons. Prove to me, says *Ariste,* that my body is nothing but pure extension and I will admit that my mind, which thinks, wills, and reasons, is neither material nor corporeal.[7] Do you not understand, replies *Théodore,* that it suffices to have extension to form a brain, a heart, arms, and hands and everything else of which your body is composed.[7] Whatever is can either be conceived alone or cannot be conceived alone. Now whatever can be conceived alone and without thought of anything else, that is, can be conceived as existing independently of everything else, is a substance.[8] And that which cannot be conceived alone or without thinking of anything else is a *maniére d'etre,* that is, a modification of substance.[9] Roundness, for example, cannot be an independent existence by itself; it always refers us to something which is round, or possesses roundness as an attribute.[9] That which is round, but is not roundness, is matter, *i. e.,* extended substance.[10] Hence extension is a substance and in no sense merely a modification or manner of being.[10] Modifications of extension consist merely in relations of distance.[11] For relations of distance can be compared, measured, and exactly determined by the principles of geometry, and it is impossible to measure in this manner our perceptions or feelings. Hence my soul is not material; it is a thinking substance, and has no resemblance to the extended substance of which my body is composed. From

[5] *Entretiens,* p 5
[6] Cf Bouillier, p 35
[7] Cf Joly, p 116ff
[8] *Entretiens,* p 6
[9] Cf Kuno Fischer, *Geschichte der neuern Philosophie,* Vol II, Ed 5, p 54
[10] Cf Bouillier, p 34
[11] *Entretiens,* p 7

this distinction Malebranche can conclude an infinity of truths; it is the foundation of the principal dogmas of philosophy.[12]

Here then we have the Cartesian distinction between extension and thought upheld in its integrity, and made the basis of a far-reaching metaphysical construction. But before we can understand this metaphysical construction, we must understand the third substance in which the two finite substances are grounded, that is, God.

Intelligible Extension and the Existence of God.

It is in the *Deuxième Entretien* that the existence of God is proved. The foundation of geometrical knowledge is intelligible extension, and infinite intelligible extension is not a modification of the finite mind.[13] It is immutable, eternal, and necessary.[13] Whatever is immutable, eternal, and necessary. and above all infinite is not created, but belongs to the creator.[13] Hence there is a God and a reason, a God in whom is found the archetype of the created world, and in whom is also found the reason which enlightens me by purely intelligible ideas. For I am sure that all men are united to the same reason that I am, since I am certain that they see or can see what I see when I enter into myself, and there discover the truths, or necessary relations, that the intelligible substance of universal reason includes.[14] Nevertheless, although it is in God that we behold intelligible extension, we only see the archetype of the material world and of an infinity of possible other worlds, we do not behold the divine essence in itself, but only in so far as it is representative of material creatures.[14] We can infer with certainty from infinite intelligible extension that God is, for nothing finite can contain an infinite reality.[14] But you do not see what God is, for God has no limits in his perfections, and what you behold when you think of immense spaces is deprived of an infinity of perfections. Thus the divine essence, in itself, escapes us.

Infinite intelligible extension, then, is only the archetype of an infinity of possible worlds like our own.[14] When we think of that extension we only behold the divine essence in so far as it is representative of bodies.[15] But when we think of being, and not of such and such beings, when we think of the infinite and not of such and such an infinite, it is certain that we do not behold so vast a reality in the modifications of our own minds.[15] For if the modifications of our own minds do not have enough

---

[12] *Entretiens*, p 8. On the distinction between mind and body, cf Novaro, p 33f
[13] *Entretiens*, p 26. Cf Ollé-Laprune, *La philosophie de Malebranche*, Vol I, p 143f
[14] *Entretiens*, p 28 Cf Kuno Fischer, *Geschichte der neuern Philosophie*, Ed. 5, Vol II, p 73
[15] *Entretiens*, p. 28. Cf. Novaro, *Die Philosophie des N Malebranche*, p 31. For Novaro, Malebranche's proof of the existence of God means *Das Sein wird gedacht —das Sein ist*

reality in them to represent infinite intelligible extension, how can they represent that which is infinite in all ways?[16] Thus only God, only the infinite, only the indeterminate being, only the infinitely infinite infinite, can contain the infinitely infinite reality which we think when we think of being.[16] Being, reality, indeterminate perfection, is not the divine substance in so far as representative of a creature.[17] It would be a contradiction were God to make or engender a being in general or being infinite in all ways that would not be identical with God himself; the Son and the Holy Spirit do not participate in the divine being; they completely receive it.[17] Again the idea of a circle in general is not the intelligible extension in so far as intelligible extension is representative of such and such a circle.[18] The idea of a circle in general covers infinite circles.[18] In the same way the idea of being without restriction, of infinity, is not the idea of creatures, but the idea that represents the divinity.[18] Being includes all things, but all things both created and possible, with all their multiplicity, cannot exhaust its vast extent.[18] God, then, is: *He that is.*[18]

But God, or the infinite, is not visible by an idea that represents him.[18] The infinite is its own idea.[18] It has no archetype.[18] It can be known, but not made, and only creatures, only such and such beings, which are "makable," are visible by the ideas that represent them.[19] We can see a circle, a house, a sun, even when such an object does not exist, for every finite object can be seen in the infinite, which includes the intelligible ideas of all things. But the infinite can only be seen by itself; nothing finite can represent it.[20] If we think of God, he exists.[20] We can contemplate the essence of a finite being without contemplating its existence; but the opposite is true of God. We can not behold his essence without admitting his existence, for he is himself his own archetype.[20] Thus the proposition, *There is a God,* is in itself the clearest of propositions affirming existence and is as certain as *I think, therefore I am.*[21]

[16] *Entretiens*, p. 28. Cf. Ollé-Laprune, *La philosophie de Malebranche,* Vol. I, p. 232ff.

[17] *Entretiens*, p. 28 and p. 29.

[18] On this point cf. Bouillier, p. 107.

[19] *Entretiens*, p. 29.

[20] *Entretiens*, p. 30.

[21] *Entretiens*, p. 30. It is interesting to observe the reaction of the modern scholastics, as ever the faithful disciples of Aristotle, to Malebranche's doctrine. Cardinal Mercier, for example, writes as follows: "The fundamental tenet of this theory is clearly belied by many psychological facts; for instance, (a) were the knowledge we have of God immediately derived from Him it would be a positive and proper knowledge, whereas our present ideas of Him are all either negative or analogical. (b) All our intellectual cognition is dependent, as we have seen, upon the senses; yet if our intellect has what is supersensible and absolute for its direct and immediate object, how has such a dependence any explanation? The theory stands also condemned by some of the consequences that may be deduced from it. For, if we enjoyed an intuition of the Divine Essence (a) we should necessarily be in possession of our highest good and complete happiness; (b) there would be no error possible about God, and (c) there would be no doubts about his existence and attributes." *Manual of Modern Scholastic Philosophy,* London, 1916, Vol. I.

There is a possibility, however, that we ourselves have created this idea of being in general or of the infinite. Perhaps the mind constructs general ideas from several particular ideas. When we have seen several trees, an apple tree, a pear tree, and a plum tree, we construct a general idea of "tree." After we have seen several beings, we construct an idea of being in general. Thus this idea of being in general may be only a confused assemblage of particular ideas.[22] If our ideas were infinite, they could not be of our own creation, but perhaps they are finite, although it is through them that we perceive the infinite.[23] The answer to this is that our ideas are finite if by ideas you understand the perceptions or modifications of our minds.[23] But if you understand by the idea of the infinite that which is the immediate object of the mind when you contemplate the infinite, assuredly that is infinite.[23] The impression that the infinite makes on the mind is finite.[23] Nevertheless, although the mind is always more touched, more penetrated, more modified by a finite idea than by the idea of the infinite, there is more reality in the idea of the infinite than in that of the finite.[23] We imagine that we have drawn our general ideas from an assemblage of particular ideas. We think of a circle of one foot diameter, then of one of a two foot diameter, then one of three, of four, and finally we do not determine the diameter at all and think of a circle in general. Now this circle in general-cannot be a confused assemblage of the particular circles of which we have thought; for it represents an infinite number of circles and we only can have thought of a finite number of circles.[24] The fact is that we find the secret of forming the idea of circle in general by seeing five or six circles. This is true in one sense and false in another. It is false that there is enough reality in the ideas of five or six circles to form the idea of circle in general. But it is true in this sense, that, after having recognized that the size of circles does not change their properties, we have perhaps ceased considering them in order and begun to consider them in general and as of indeterminate quantity.[24] We could not form general ideas if we did not find in the idea of the infinite sufficient reality to give generality to our ideas.[24] You can only think of an indeterminate diameter because you see the infinite in extension, that is, that you can augment or diminish a diameter to infinity.[25] Without the idea of the infinite, you could think only of such and such a particular circle but never of a circle in general.[25] No finite and determinate idea can represent anything of the infinite and indeterminate, but the mind, with-

[22] *Entretiens*, p 33
[23] *Entretiens* ɪ 34
[24] *Entretiens*, 35
[25] *Entretiens.* 36

out reflection, joins to its finite ideas the idea of a generality that it finds in the infinite.[25]

Thus a mere confused assemblage of particular ideas can never possess true generality. If we mix twenty colors together, we do not obtain color in general, but some particular color.[26] If we mix feelings to obtain a feeling in general we fail in the same way.[26] Every modification of the mind is, as the modification of a particular being, itself a particular thing, and is unable to possess true generality.[26] We must not suppose that because modifications are more sensible than ideas that they are more real.[27] Such a judgment is like that of people who say that there is more matter in a cubic foot of lead than in a cubic foot of air.[27] This is to give the prick of a pin more reality than the whole universe and the infinite being itself.[28] In this way, Malebranche answers the empiricist, who would reduce our ideas to mere heaps of sensations, and thus defends his idea of God.[29]

In the *Troisème Entretien* Malebranche explains how the divine Word as universal reason includes in its substance the primordial ideas of all created and possible things.[30] All intelligences are united to this sovereign reason and discover in it ideas according as God wills.[30] Thus, we cannot doubt that intelligible extension, which is the archetype of bodies, is contained in the universal reason which enlightens all minds and even him with whom it is consubstantial.[30] Thus there is a profound difference between *"la lumière de nos idées"* and *"les ténebres de ses propres modifications."*[30] It is this difference that is the basis of the ontological argument for the existence of God as expounded by Malebranche.[31]

It is the distinction between intelligible and material extension that distinguishes the system of Malebranche from that of Spinoza. This comes out in the very interesting correspondence between Malebranche and de Mairan, a well-instructed and skillful student of both Malebranche and Spinoza.[32] De Mairan, as Kuno Fischer says,[33] turns to Malebranche for aid in withstanding the attraction of Spinozistic pantheism. Malebranche had spoken of a fundamental error in the system of Spinoza; will he not make it clear just what this error is? Malebranche replies that Spinoza has not adequately distinguished between intelligible and real extension, between the world in God and the created world. The world of eternal ideas is, of course, *necessary* in character; created extension or real space— what Spinoza called an attribute of God—is not necessary but

---

[26] *Entretiens*, p. 37.
[27] *Entretiens*, p. 38.
[28] *Entretiens*, p. 39.
[29] On this whole matter *cf.* Bouillier, p. 74.
[30] *Entretiens*, p. 42-43.
[31] Cf. Joly, p. 55f and p. 60f.
[32] Cf. Victor Cousin, *Fragments de philosophie cartésienne*.
[33] *Geschichte de neuern Philosophie*, Vol. II, p. 86.

contingent in character. Like all created beings, it is a product of the free act of God. As Joly remarks,[34] this *apercu*—that is, the distinction between intelligible and material extension—does sufficiently distinguish Malebranche from Spinoza. On the one hand, the transcendent God, on the other, the immanent God. The discussion between de Mairan and Malebranche develops many interesting and instructive points. Unfortunately the limits of the present study prevent the exposition here

It is interesting to compare this demonstration of the existence of God with the arguments of Descartes Descartes uses three arguments. The first is from the idea of God to the cause of the idea of God which can only be God himself. "There is no doubt," he says, "that those (ideas) which represent to me substances are something more and contain so to speak more objective reality within them (that is to say, by representation participate in a higher degree of being or perfection) than those that simply represent modes and accidents ; and that idea again by which I understand a supreme God, eternal, infinite, immutable, omniscient, omnipotent, and creator of all things which are outside of himself, has certainly more objective reality in itself than those ideas by which finite substances are represented Now it is evident by the natural light that there must at least be as much reality in the efficient and total cause as in its effect."[35] Therefore there must be a God since otherwise we should have no idea of him. The second argument is essentially a restatement of the first. What, less than God, can be the cause of the existence of me who contain in myself the idea of God?[36] The third argument, which Descartes says has the appearance of being a sophism,[37] is the Ontological Argument in its purest form. "But when I think of it with more attention, I clearly see that existence can no more be separated from the essence of God than can its having three angles equal to two right angles be separated from the essence of a rectilinear triangle, or the idea of a mountain from the idea of a valley, and so there is not any less repugnance to our conceiving a God (that is, a being supremely perfect) to whom existence is lacking, (that is to say, to whom a certain perfection is lacking) than to conceive of a mountain which has no valley."[38]

It is, of course, only with this third argument that Malebranche's argument is to be compared. We immediately behold the essence and existence of the divine being and discern that they are inseparable. Spinoza's arguments are virtually the same. The *Ethics*[39] defines God as "a being absolutely infinite—

[34] Joly, p 81
[35] *Meditations, Philosophical Works*, Trans Ross and Haldane, p 162
[36] *Meditations, Op cit*, pp. 167 171.
[37] *Op cit*, p 118
[38] *Op cit*, p. 181
[39] *Chief Works of Benedict de Spinoza*, trans by R H M Elwes, Vol II

that is, a substance consisting in infinite attributes, of which each expresses eternal and infinite essentiality."[40] Proposition XI establishes the conclusion that "God, or substance, consisting of infinite attributes, of which each expresses eternal and infinite essentiality, necessarily exists," because, as Proposition VII states, "Existence belongs to the nature of substance."

Many a proposition of the *Ethics* might have been written by Malebranche. Consider, for example, the following, Proposition XIII: "Substance, absolutely infinite, is indivisible." Proposition XV: "Whatever is, is in God, and without God nothing can be or be conceived." Proposition XVII: "God acts solely by the laws of his own nature and is not disturbed by any one." Proposition XX: "The existence of God and his essence are one and the same." Proposition XXIV: "The essence of things produced by God does not involve existence." Proposition XXV: "God is the efficient cause not only of the existence of things but of their essence." Proposition XXX: "Intellect in function finite or in function infinite, must comprehend the attributes of God and the modifications of God and nothing else." Proposition XXXI: "The intellect in function, whether finite or infinite, as will, desire, love, should be referred to passive nature and not to active nature." These propositions show how the two systems tend to coincide, although the radical difference between a transcendent and an immanent God is never to be lost sight of.[41]

Occasionalism.[42]

In the *Quatriéme Entretien* Malebranche discusses the nature of sense, the wisdom of the laws of the union of the soul and the body, and the fact that this union was changed into dependence by the sin of the first man.[43] In speaking of the nature of sense he adds nothing to what we have not already brought out in our review of the *Recherche.* The chief point is the subjectivity of sensible qualities.[44] But in the next division of the dialogue he expounds the very important doctrine of occasionalism as an explanation of the relation between mind and body. When we investigate the reason of certain effects, and ascend from effect to cause we come in the end to a general cause, or to a cause which one clearly sees has no relation to the effect that it produces, and then, in place of constructing chimeras, we must have recourse to the author of nature. If

[40] Part I, Def. 6.

[41] There thus seems to be some exaggeration in Hegel's statement that *"Die Philosophie des Malebranche hat ganz denselben Inhalt alader Spinozismus, aber in anderer, theologisher Form."* *Geschichte der Philosophie, Werke,* 1844, XV, p. 369. On the relation between Malebranche and Spinoza, *cf.* Kuno Fischer, *Geschichte der neuern Philosophie,* Vol. II, Ed. 5, p. 80f.

[42] On the whole matter of occasionalism *cf.* Novaro, *op. cit.,* p. 43.

[43] *Entretiens,* p. 69.

[44] *Entretiens* p. 76 77. Cf. Kuno Fischer, *Op. cit.,* p 54.

you ask me the cause of the pain that we feel when we are
pricked, I should be wrong in answering at once that it is one
of the laws of the author of nature that being pricked is followed by pain. I should first tell you that the fibers of our flesh
cannot be separated without disturbing our nerves which reach
to the brain, and without disturbing the brain itself. But if you
wish to know whence it comes about that when a certain part of
my brain is disturbed in this way, I feel the pain of being
pricked, we can assign no further natural or particular cause
but must refer to the author of nature.[44] We clearly see that
there can be no necessary connection between the disturbances
of the brain and the feelings of the soul; therefore, we must
have recourse to a power which is not contained in these two
beings.[45] There is no metamorphosis of physical event into physical event. The disturbance of the brain cannot change itself
into a mental state.[45]—When we press the corner of the eye, you
see light. this is because he who alone can act upon minds has
established certain laws according to which body and soul re-
ciprocally correspond to each other.[46] You see a light where
there is no luminous body because luminous bodies act in a similar way on the nervous system and the brain, and God acts according to constant laws.[47] God performs no miracles, says
Malebranche in this connection.[48] His conduct always bears the
character of his attributes, it remains forever the same, unless
in some circumstances, his immutability is a lesser consideration
as compared with some other of his perfections.[48] God does not
stand *"les bras croisés;"* everything that happens in the world
is an expression of his activity.[49] There is no necessary connec-

---

[44] Cardinal Mercier, in the work cited above, offers the following criticism of
occasionalism "If I consider myself acting, I become conscious of two things first,
that my act is real, and, secondly, that until it is over and done with it is thoroughly
dependent upon me " "If we study the things of nature we see a marvelous variety of
type, in internal constitution and in function Now what is all this profuse variety
in their natures for, if they are not efficient causes? Such richness would be pur-
poseless and a meaningless prodigality" *Op cit,* Vol I, p 540 Furthermore, "occasionalism compromises free will," (p 540), "leads to idealism," (p 540) and to
"pantheism" (p 540)

[46] *Entretiens,* p 78 Thus Leibniz's famous figure of the clock-maker, who was
obliged continually to readjust his clocks to keep them running together, is a very in-
accurate description of occasionalism This conception of God's action taking place
according to universal decrees, and not according to particular decrees, is one of Malebranche's most important theological positions The difference between Leibniz's pre-
established harmony and Malebranche's occasionalism is very nearly one of names, for
both thinkers believed in an immutable God, who foresees everything, and rules everything according to an unchanging will We are sorry to note that Mr Russell, in his
scholarly *Philosophy of Leibniz,* accepts Leibniz's misinterpretation of Malebranche
Russell says "The advantage which he (Leibniz) had over occasionalism, and of
which he made the most, was that by the activity of every substance he was able to
preserve the harmony of all the series, without the perpetual intervention of God
This advantage was already secured in Spinoza, but not in occasionalism such as that
of Malebranche" (p 136f) One hour's reading of Malebranche would have convinced Mr Russell of the contrary.

[47] *Entretiens,* p 79
[48] *Entretiens,* p 80
[49] *Entretiens,* p 80

tion between the two substances of which we are composed [49]
There is no relation of causality from body to mind or from
mind to body.[50] God ceaselessly wills that certain disturbances
of the brain be always joined with certain thoughts, and it is
this constant and efficacious will of the creator that produces the
union of the two substances.[50] —

Why did God will to join mind and body? The answer is,
apparently, that God wished to give us as he gave to his Son, a
victim which we could offer to him [50] He wished to make us
merit, by sacrifice and self-annihilation, the possession of eternal
goods.[50] For this reason we have our bodies. That our bodily
life might be conserved and at the same time our souls directed
as far as possible upon eternal goods, God has established as an
occasional cause of the confused knowledge we have of the presence of objects, and of their properties in relation to us, not the
activity of attention, but diverse disturbances in our brains.[51]
He has given us distinct witnesses, not of the nature and properties of the bodies that surround us, but of their relation to our
own bodies, to the end that we be able to work with success for
the conservation of our lives without being incessantly attentive
to our needs.[51] We are, however, subordinated to our bodies to
the extent that we are by reason of the original sin [52] That a
prick warn me is just and conformable to order, but that it
should trouble me, make me unhappy, disturb my ideas and
prevent me from thinking of true goods, is a disorder, and is
unworthy of the wisdom and goodness of the creator.[53] The
explanation is that the human spirit has lost before God its dig-
nity and excellence; we are sinners worthy of the divine wrath.[54]

Image and Meaning.

The *Cinquième Entretien* discusses the use of the senses in
science, the distinction between clear ideas and confused feeling, and the fact that the idea illumines the mind, while it is
by feeling (*sentiment*) that the intelligible idea becomes sensible.[55] It will not be necessary to dwell very long on this dialogue since the main ideas have already been brought out in our
earlier discussion. We may content ourselves with noting an
admirably clear statement of the relation between image and
meaning, to use the language of modern psychology It is not
sense, but reason joined to sense, that enlightens us and discloses
the truth to us.[56] It is the clear idea of extension and not black
and white which are only feelings, only confused modalities of
sense, that gives mathematical truth [56] In our perception of

[50] *Entretiens,* p 81
[51] *Entretiens,* p. 84
[52] *En , et ,* p. 88
[53] *Entretiens* p. 87
[54] *Entretiens,* p 88
[55] *Entretiens,* p 96
[56] *Entretiens,* p 100

sensible objects there is always a clear idea and a confused feeling; the idea represents their essence, the feeling informs us of their existence [56] The first gives us their nature, properties, and relation among themselves, the second the relation they bear to the convenience and conservation of life.[56] But as a whole this dialogue adds very little to what we have learned from the *Recherche*

The Existence of Bodies.

The *Sixième Entretien*, on the contrary, on proofs of the existence of bodies drawn from revelation, on the two sorts of revelation, and upon natural revelation as an occasion of error, is relatively important.[57]

There are sciences of two sorts: One sort considers the relations of ideas; the other, the relations of things by means of their ideas.[58] The first sort are evident in every way; the second are only evident on the supposition that things resemble the ideas we have of them and according to which we reason.[58] These latter sciences are very useful but they involve great obscurity, for they presuppose facts concerning which it is impossible to know the exact truth. But if we can find some means of assuring ourselves of the truth of our suppositions, we can avoid error and at the same time discover truths which more closely concern us.[59] Thus the best use that we can make of our *of* minds is to discover what things are related to us, what things can make us happy and perfect.[59] Thus it seems that the best use we can make of our minds is to attempt to understand the truths which we believe by faith.[59] We believe these great truths, but that does not dispense those who can from filling their minds with them and convincing themselves of them in all possible ways.[59] For faith is given us to regulate all the movements of our minds as well as those of our hearts.[60] It is given us to lead us to the understanding of those very truths it teaches.[60]

A man must be a good philosopher to enter into the truths of faith, and the stronger one is in the truths of religion the stronger one is in metaphysics.[61] Good philosophers can not

[57] *Entretiens*, p 120
[58] *Entretiens*, p 122
[59] *Entretiens*, p 123
[60] *Entretiens*, p. 124
[61] *Entretiens*, p 125 Of Bouillier, p 139, and E Boutroux, *L'intellectualisme de Malebranche, Revue de Metaphysique et de Morale*, Vol XXIII, pp 27-36 In this last paper it is shown that Malebranche, although an intellectualist, was obliged to extend his intellectualism beyond the limits of mathematical truth and make it include religious and moral truth Thus Boutroux says· "Etant donnée l'impossibilité de reduire a l'intelligible mathematique une partie considérable des choses que nous tenons pour des realités, telles que l'existence du monde matériel et les vérites morales et religieuses deux partis sont possible ou tenter de demontrer que ces éléments refractaires ne possedent aucune réalité effective, et ne sont que des fantomes de notre imagination, ou se demander si l'intelligence mathematique est bien toute l'intelligence, si l'intelligence ne comporterait pas des modes de penser et de comprendre, analogues, mais supérieurs a la démonstration mathématique. De cette alternative, Malebranche adopte le second terme" (p 85).

have opinions opposed to those of true Christians.[62] For whether Jesus Christ, the Word, eternal reason, speaks to philosophers in their most secret souls, or whether he instructs Christians by the visible authority of the Church, he cannot contradict himself.[62] Truth speaks in various ways, but it always says the same thing.[62] We must not oppose philosophy to religion, unless indeed it is the false philosophy of the pagans, which does not bear the stamp of truth, that invincible evidence which compels all attentive minds to submit.[62]

Now there are three sorts of beings of which we can have knowledge: God, or the infinitely perfect being; minds, that we only know by our inner feeling of our own souls; and bodies, the existence of which we are assured of by a revelation.[63] For it is only by revelation that we know of the existence of bodies.[64] It is God himself who produces in our souls all the different feelings by which they are affected on the occasion of changes in our bodies in accordance with the general laws governing the union of body and soul.[64] These laws are nothing but the constant and efficacious decrees of the creator.[64] Thus it is God himself who reveals to us what takes place outside of us.[64] But perhaps there are no external bodies? Is the revelation that God gives us of their existence certain? It is certain that we see certain bodies which do not exist, as for example when we sleep or fever disturbs our brains.[65] If God in consequence of his general laws sometimes gives us deceptive perceptions, could he not always give them to us? Thus it seems that we should suspend our judgment on the existence of bodies.[65]

It is true that no exact demonstration of the existence of bodies can be given.[65] On the contrary it is possible to give an exact demonstration that such a demonstration is impossible.[65] For the notion of an infinitely perfect being includes no necessary relation to any creature.[66] God is fully self-sufficient.[66] Matter is not a necessary emanation from the divinity, whence it follows that no demonstration of the existence of matter is possible.[66] The existence of bodies is arbitrary; this divine resolution is not like the decrees involving the punishment of the wicked and the compensation of good works. These latter decrees of God and many others like them are necessarily included in the divine reason, that substantial law which is the inviolable rule of all the decrees of the infinitely perfect being and generally of all intelligences.[66] The will to create bodies is not necessarily included in the notion of a being infinitely perfect;

---

[62] *Entretiens*, p. 125. On Malebranche's theory of the relation of faith and reason, see Ollé-Laprune, *La philosophie de Malebranche*, Vol. I, p. 100ff. *Cf.* also Joly, p. 149ff.
  [63] *Entretiens*, p. 126.
  [64] *Entretiens*, p. 127.
  [65] *Entretiens*, p. 128.
  [66] *Entretiens*, p. 129.

rather this notion seems to exclude such a will.[66] Only revelation can assure us that God did indeed will to create bodies. There are two sorts of revelation, natural and supernatural.[67] The former take place according to certain general laws which are known to us, and the latter either according to certain unknown general laws, or by particular volitions superadded to the general laws.[67] Now both revelations are in themselves authentic.[67] But natural revelation is now an occasion of error, not because in itself it is false but because in the first place we do not make the proper use of it, and secondly because original sin has corrupted our natures.[67] The general rules of the union of mind and body are very wisely established.[67] Whence, then, comes it that we are now plunged in an infinity of errors? It is because our minds are obscured, because our union with universal reason is greatly enfeebled by the dependence upon our bodies in which our sin has placed us[68] As God follows and ought to follow exactly the laws he has established concerning the union of the two natures of which we are composed, and as we have lost the power that our rebellious animal spirits make in the brain, we mistake phantoms for realities.[69] But the cause of our error is not precisely the falsity of the natural revelation, but rather the impudence and temerity of our judgments, in a word, the disorder into which sin has thrown us.[69] Nevertheless there is no good reason for doubting the existence of bodies in general.[69] We see that the errors into which we fall concerning bodies are merely because the irregularity of our conduct cannot influence the uniformity of divine action[69] Therefore, although we may be mistaken concerning the existence of such and such a body, we need not doubt concerning the existence of bodies in general. For the different feelings we have of them are so consecutive, so chained together and so well ordered, that it appears certain that God would have to have willed to deceive us were nothing of all that we see real.[70]

But it is faith that gives an irresistible demonstration which cannot be resisted; for whether or not there are bodies, it is certain that we see them and that it is God alone who gives us these perceptions[70] God, then, presents to my mind these appearances of men, these books, these preachers, I read in the New Testament of the miracles of the Man-God, of his resurrection, of his ascension to heaven, of the preaching of the apostles, of its fortunate success and of the establishment of the Church.[70] I compare all these appearances with my ideas of God, of the beauty of religion, of the sanctity of morality, and of the necessity of a cult; and at length I am led to believe all that faith

[67] *Entretiens*, p 131
[68] *Entretiens*, p 133
[69] *Entretiens*, p 134
[70] *Entretiens*, p 135

teaches.[70] I believe it without having a demonstrative proof of it, for nothing seems more unreasonable than infidelity.[70] Men need an authority to teach them truths necessary to lead them to their end.[70] Now faith teaches that God created the heavens and the earth, and teaches me that the Holy Scripture is a divine book. This book tells me directly and positively that there are thousands and thousands of creatures.[71] Hence my "appearances" change into "realities."[71] Thus Malebranche retires before subjective idealism in the name of Christian faith.[72]

---

[71] *Entretiens*, p. 136.

[72] On this matter *cf.* Joly, 126ff. For a special study of the problem *cf.* the existence of an outer world in Malebranche's system *cf.* Pillon, *L'évolution de l'idéalisme au dix-huitiéme siécle, Malebranche et ses critiques, Année philosophique*, No. 4, p. 108. Pillon is himself a subjective idealist (*Cf.*, p. 206) and he is interested in showing the relation of Malebranche's doctrine to his own position. Since our aim is merely to present the doctrine in its original form, we have not given any account of Pillon's paper, which, valuable as it is in itself, adds very little to our knowledge of what Malebranche himself thought.

CHAPTER VII MALEBRANCHE'S METAPHYSICS AND

THEOLOGY (Continued)

The Divine Omnipotence

The *Septième Entretien* is on the inefficacy of natural causes, or the powerlessness of creatures, and on the proposition that it is only to God that we are directly and immediately united.[1] As we have already seen neither mind nor matter can affect the other.[2] Neither can body act on body.[3] It is contradictory to suppose that such action is possible A body cannot move itself.[4] This is evident from the pure essence of matter, intelligible extension.[5] Now a body must be either in rest or motion, and it is self-contradictory for a body to be in neither rest nor motion.

The same will that created bodies always subsists, and should this will cease to exist, bodies would necessarily cease to exist.[6] It is, then, this same will that puts bodies in rest or motion, for it gives them existence, and, as existing, they must be in either rest or motion.[6] Hence it is self-contradictory that God should make a body and not give it either rest or motion.[6] It is supposed that when the moment of creation is past, God no longer gives bodies their rest or motion; but the moment of creation never passes.[6] Should God cease to will that there be a world, the world would be annihilated, for the world depends on the will of the creator.[7] The conservation of creatures is only their continued creation.[7] When a human architect dies, the house he has built may remain, but we depend essentially upon the creator.[7] Since bodies depend essentially upon the creator, they only exist as sustained by his continual influence, and thus whatever takes place in the world is only an expression of divine activity.[8] The greatest, most fertile and most necessary of principles is that God does not communicate his power to creatures and only unites them with each other by making their modalities occasional causes of effects he himself produces.[9] One moving ball does not move another upon collision; for one body can only communicate its motion to another body by communi-

[1] *Entretiens*, p 141   Cf Ollé-Laprune, *op cit*, Vol I, p 321ff
[2] *Entretiens*, p 144f.
[3] *Entretiens*, p 149
[4] *Entretiens*, p 150f
[5] *Entretiens*, p 151
[6] *Entretiens*, p 152 Cf Bouillier, p 116f
[7] *Entretiens*, p 153
[8] *Entretiens*, p 155. Cf Kuno Fischer, *op cit*, p 56
[9] *Entretiens*, p 158

eating its moving force; but the moving force of a moving body
is not a quality that belongs to the body but is the will of the
creator which successively sustains it in existence in different
places.[10]

Thus creatures are united only to God, and depend directly
and essentially upon him.[11] We have nothing that comes from
our own nature, or from the imaginary Nature of the philosophers, but everything comes from God.[12] God himself is present in the midst of us, not as a simple spectator, but as the
principle of our society, the bond of our friendship, and the
soul of our commerce.[12]

It is interesting to observe that Hume's rejection of Malebranche's theory is a consequence of his dictum that all knowledge comes from impressions. In the *Treatise*, for example,
Hume says: "Matter, they (the Cartesians) say, is entirely
unactive, and depriv'd of any power, by which it may produce
or continue or communicate motion. But since these effects are
evident to our senses, and since the power that produces them
must be placed somewhere, it must lie in the Deity, or that
divine being, who contains in his nature all excellency and perfection. . . . This opinion is certainly very curious, and well
worth our attention; but 'twill appear superfluous to examine
it in this place if we reflect a moment on our present purpose in
taking notice of it. We have established it as a principle, that
as all ideas are derived from impressions, or some precedent
perceptions, 'tis impossible we can have any idea of power and
efficacy, unless some instances can be produced, wherein this
power *is perceived* to exert itself. Now, as these instances can
never be discovered in body, the *Cartesians*, proceeding upon
their principle of innate ideas, have had recourse to a supreme
spirit or deity, whom they consider as the only active being in
the universe, and as the immediate cause of every alteration in
matter. But the principle of innate ideas being allowed to be
false, it follows that the supposition of a deity can serve us in
no stead, in accounting for that idea of agency, which we search
for in vain in all the objects which are presented to our senses,
or which we are internally conscious of in our own minds. For,
if every idea be derived from an impression, the idea of a deity
proceeds from the same origin; and if no impression either of
sensation or reflection, implies any force or efficacy, 'tis equally
impossible to discover in such a principle; the same course of
reasoning should determine them to exclude it from the supreme
being."[13] This passage sets the relation of Hume to Malebranche
in a clear light. It is maintained by Dr. Doxsee[14] that Hume

[10] *Entretiens*, p. 159.
[11] *Entretiens*, p. 164.
[12] *Entretiens*, p. 165.
[13] *Hume's Treatise on Human Nature*, Ed. Green and Grose, 1886, p. 454.
[14] *Philosophical Review*, Vol. XXV, pp. 692-701.

and Malebranche make "a very similar analysis of causation."[15] There is a good deal of truth in this position, but yet as Dr. Doxsee himself says, "Although Malebranche remarkably anticipates the position that was later to be developed by Hume, the final place of causation in his system is by no means what the analysis just outlined would seem to indicate All the causal efficacy that he denies to finite creatures he attributed to God."[16] The difference between Malebranche and Hume remains as radical as the difference between a rationalist and empiricist must always be. For Malebranche, we must remember, has no occasion to deny causality in principle, as Hume was forced to; on the contrary, his philosophy merely focuses causality in a supreme cause without questioning the validity of the concept itself.

The Attributes of God.

The *Huitième Entretien*, on God and his attributes, develops the same theme. By Divinity we understand the infinite, being without restriction, the infinitely perfect being[17] We know that he exists by the thought of him.[17] God is independent, hence he is immutable.[18] He cannot be affected by outer causes, hence, should he change, he must needs change himself.[18] But although God is absolutely free, he does not change himself.[18] God forms his eternal decrees according to his eternal wisdom, which is the inviolable rule of his actions, and although the effects of these decrees are infinite and they produce thousands and thousands of changes in the universe, they are themselves unchanging.[19] But how can God be both free and immutable? The answer is that in God there is no succession of thoughts and volitions. By an eternal and immutable act he knows and wills all that he knows and wills. He wills with perfect liberty and entire indifference to create the world; but his decrees assumed, they cannot be changed [19] They are not absolutely necessary, but necessary by the force of the supposition.[20] Certain of his decrees only hold for a limited time; these are those concerning miracles. When that time arrives, he does not change his mind, for these special decrees have been included in that eternal act of will which is related to all the times he includes in his eternity.[20]

God, then, is all-powerful, eternal, necessary and immense He is immense because the divine substance is everywhere, in the universe and beyond it [21] God's work is contained in him, but he is not contained in his work [21] It is because he is not

[15] Doxsee, *op cit*, p 692
[16] *Op cit*, p. 699
[17] *Entretiens*, p 174
[18] *Entretiens*, p 175
[19] *Entretiens*, p 176
[20] *Entretiens*, p 177
[21] *Entretiens*, p 179

corporeal that he is everywhere.[21] Were he corporeal he could
not penetrate bodies as he does.[21] The divine substance does
not possess local extension and is not more present in an ele-
phant than in a fly.[22] Created extension is to the divine immensity as time is to eternity   There is neither past nor future
in his existence, and in the same way, there is in his substance
neither great nor small but everything is simple, equal and infinite.[22] God's existence is completely in eternity, and completely in every moment of his eternity, in the same way God is not
partly in the sky and partly in the earth, but he is completely
in his immensity, and completely in every body that is extended in his immensity, he is completely contained in every
part of matter although matter is infinitely divisible. God is
extended since he contains in himself all perfections, but he is
not extended like bodies.[23]

But the divine immensity is not to be confused with intelligible extension.[24] The immensity of God is the fact that his
substance is everywhere without local extension.[25] But intelligible extension is only the substance of God in so far as his substance is representative of bodies. It is the idea or archetype
of bodies.[26] No finite mind can understand the immensity of
God, but on the other hand nothing is more clear than intelligible extension.[26] In fact, extension is an attribute that is totally inadequate to the divine essence   The property of the
infinite that is unintelligible to the human mind is that it is at
the same time one and all things, composed of an infinity of perfections, and so simple that each perfection it contains includes
all the others without any real distinction[27] This property is
more in agreement with the nature of the soul, which, without
any composition of parts, receives at the same time different
modalities, than it is with that of extension.[27] Thus there is no
substance more imperfect and more removed from the divinity
than matter.[27]

That "impious man" of Malebranche's own time, Spinoza,
who made the universe his God, had in truth no God and was a
veritable atheist.[29] On the other hand, many good people have

---

[21] *Entretiens*, p 180, and *cf.* Bouillier, p 109
[22] *Entretiens*, p 180
[23] *Entretiens*, p 184
[24] As Bouillier remarks, Malebranche was accused by Arnauld of making God
corporeal and of deifying the material universe   In a word, he was accused of Spi-
noaism   *Cf* Bouillier, p 49   But as a matter of fact, as Bouillier says, Malebranche
places extension in God, not *formaliter*, but *eminenter*   And, as we have seen, it is
by the distinction between intelligible and material extension that he answers de Mai
ran   *Cf* Bouillier, p 51, and Joly, p 79, as well as M Ginsberg, *The Nature of
Knowledge as conceived by Malebranche, Proceedings of the Aristotelian Society,*
1916-17, p 174
[25] *Entretiens*, p 186
[26] *Entretiens*, p. 187
[27] *Entretiens*, p. 188
[29] *Entretiens*, p 189   *Cf* Bouillier, p 106   On Malebranche and Spinoza consult P Janet, *Le Spinozisme en France, Revue Philosophique*, p 110f, 1882

an unworthy idea of the divinity. They regard God as the creator of the universe and as nothing more; we cannot avoid complaining of the idea they form of the infinite being. Men humanize all things, and strip the infinitely perfect being of all his essential attributes.[29]

If we consult the idea of an infinitely perfect being, we see that omniscience is involved in it.[30] God knows in himself all that He knows.[31] He is not only wise but is wisdom itself, not only enlightenment but the light that enlightens.[31] It is by this wisdom that one of us sees what another sees I see that two plus two are four, and I am certain that God sees this and that all minds either actually do or are able to see this.[31] There is, however, this great difference between finite minds and the mind of God, God is wise by His own wisdom, and we are wise by union with His wisdom [32] The question may be asked whether, when God sees that two plus two is four, and at the same time two persons behold the same truth, may there not be, not one truth which all three minds behold, but three similar truths? On the contrary, there are three similar perceptions of one and the same truth. And we know that the perceptions are similar, because we know that one and the same truth is perceived.[33] Thus God is not only the efficient cause of our knowledge, but also the formal cause.[33]

Justice is also an attribute of the divinity. God includes in the simplicity of his being ideas of all things and of their infinite relations.[33] We can distinguish in God two sorts of truths, relations of magnitude and relations of perfection, speculative and practical truths, relations which arouse judgments by reason of their evidence and relations which furthermore excite movements.[34] Twice two is four, and a man is worth more than an animal; in the first, we have a speculative truth or relation of magnitude, in the second, we have a relation of perfection.[34] God knows and loves all that he includes within the simplicity of His being, and he loves everything in proportion to its perfection or according as it is lovable [34] He loves the immutable order which consists of the relations of perfection. He is thus essentially just. He cannot positively and directly will that any disorder occur in His works, for he esteems all creatures according to the perfections of their archetypes.[34]

God is neither good, nor merciful, nor patient, as these things are commonly understood.[35] Such ideas are unworthy of the infinitely perfect being.[35] Nevertheless he regards good

[30] *Entretiens*, p 191
[31] *Entretiens*, p 192.
[33] *Entretiens*, p. 193
[33] *Entretiens*, p 194 Bouillier makes it clear that without the presupposition of a universal truth we are forced into skepticism, p 63. On the eternal truths cf Ollé-Laprune, Vol I, pp 208ff
[34] *Entretiens* p 195
[35] *Entretiens*, p 198

works and punishes those who offend him.[35] God does not depend upon us; and is completely self-sufficient.[36] Our minds are without wills save in so far as God ceaselessly impresses upon us a natural and irresistible love of the good.[36] God only acts in us because he wills to act in us according to his love of himself and of his divine perfections.[37] He can not will that our love which is the effect of his own be directed upon the less lovable in the place of the more lovable. He wills that the immutable Order be our law. Since he has made us free to follow or not to follow that Order we can be punished and rewarded.[37] The sinner does not offend God as one man offends another, nor does God punish him for the sake of the pleasure of vengeance, but God punishes him because he cannot act otherwise than according to the immutable order of his perfections.[37] God is always severe, always an exact observer of the eternal laws.[38]

The Theory of Providence.

The *Neuvième Entretien* develops further the theory of Providence. First of all, the errors of pantheism must be refuted. It is supposed that the infinitely perfect being can will nothing, and that we are ourselves a necessary emanation from the Divinity.[39] Malebranche finds it difficult to believe that there have been philosophers who really held this view.[40] Even the author who revived this impiety (Spinoza) agrees that God is an infinitely perfect being.[41] And if this is true, how could created things be only parts and modifications of the divinity? Is it perfection to be unjust in his parts, unhappy, ignorant, brutal, impious? There are more sinners than virtuous people; more idolaters than believers; what a conflict between the divinity and his own parts! A God necessarily hated, blasphemed, and unknown by the greater part of what he is! A God avenging himself upon himself, an infinitely perfect being composed of all the disorders of the universe![42]

The question inevitably arises, however, as to why the infinitely perfect being created us when he had no need of us. How could a being to whom nothing was lacking will anything? The infinitely perfect being necessarily loves his own perfections; the movement of his love cannot lead Him elsewhere.[43] In God any other love besides love for himself would be a lawless love.[44] We can say that God created us out of pure goodness, but only

---

[35] *Entretiens*, p. 199.
[37] *Entretiens*, p. 200.
[38] *Entretiens*, p. 201. On the attributes of God in Malebranche's system, see Ollé-Laprune. *La philosophie de Malebranche*, Vol. I, p. 357ff.
[39] *Entretiens*, p. 205.
[40] *Entretiens*, p. 206.
[41] Malebranche calls Spinoza a *veritable athée* (*Entretiens, VIII*) and a *misérable* (*Méditations metaphysique et chrétiennes, IX*). Cf. Bouillier, p. 33 and p. 35.
[42] *Entretiens*, p. 206.
[43] *Entretiens*, p. 207.
[44] *Entretiens*, p. 208.

in the sense that he had no need of us.[44] But we were made for him and the motive and end of his decrees can only be found in himself.[44] In what sense may God be said to have created the world for his glory? When an architect has made a building of excellent architecture he takes a secret satisfaction in it, for the work witnesses the skill of his art.[45] Thus one can say that the beauty of his work does him honor, because it bears the character of the qualities he esteems and loves.[45] When a second person contemplates the work of the architect and admires the proportions, the architect draws therefrom a second glory which is chiefly founded on the love and admiration he has of his own qualities as an architect.[46] Now God loves his own qualities and his work which expresses these attributes thus glorifies him, as the work of the architect glorifies *him*. Whether or not men honor the works of God as they should, he draws eternal glory from them.[46] Nevertheless this glory would not be enough to determine him to act, unless there were something divine and infinite in the world itself.[47] The universe, however great, however perfect it may be, in so far as it is finite is unworthy of a God whose worth is infinite.[47] Now only union with a divine person can render the world worthy of being created by a divine being.[47] God foresaw and permitted the original sin; this proves that a universe redeemed by Jesus Christ is better than a universe without sin.[48] The Incarnation of the Word in Jesus Christ first renders the world worthy of its creator.[49]

But why did God wait for an eternity before creating the world? It is because he must leave the finite creature the essential marks of finitude; now the great mark of dependence is to have not existed. An eternal world would appear as a necessary emanation from the divinity.[50] God draws from the world, through Jesus Christ, a glory that satisfies him, but were this glory eternal, it would offend his attributes, which He must always respect.[50]

The Explanation of Evil.

It is in this same *Neuvième Entretien* that Malebranche formulates his theory of Providence in so far as it is an explanation of evil.[51] God did not wish to make his work as perfect as possible without regard to the ways in which he made it, but as perfect as possible in relation to ways that are worthy of him.[52] What God absolutely wills is to act always in the most divine

---

[45] *Entretiens*, p 209
[44] *Entretiens*, p 210
[47] *Entretiens*, p 211.
[48] *Entretiens*, p 212
[49] *Entretiens*, p 214
[50] *Entretiens*, p 216   Cf Bouillier, p 117f, Joly, p 87f, and p 165f
[51] On Arnauld's criticism of Malebranche's theory of Providence, *cf Ollé-Laprune*, Vol II, pp 42ff
[52] *Entretiens*, p 223.

fashion that he can.[52]   God sees from all eternity all possible
works and all possible ways to produce each one of them, and
as he acts only for his own glory, only according to what he is,
he is determined to choose the work which can be produced and
conserved by ways which, joined to this work, honor him more
than any other works produced by any other ways.[52]   Not only
his work but his ways must bear the character of his attributes.[53]
If a world more perfect than ours could only be created and
conserved by less perfect ways, God is too wise and loves his
glory too well, to prefer this to the universe he has created.[53]   A
world more perfect but produced by ways less simple and fertile
would not bear as much as ours the character of the divine attributes.[54]   This is why the world is full of impious persons, of monsters, of disorders of all kinds.[54]   He not only permits monsters;
he positively creates them.[54]   But he creates them out of respect
for the universality of his ways.[54]   In this way we can conceive
that all these effects that contradict each other, all these works
which conflict and destroy each other, all these disorders which
disfigure the universe, are not in contradiction with their governing cause, and show no want of intelligence, and no impo-
tence, but a prodigious fecundity and perfect uniformity in the
laws of nature.[55]

Divine Will and Divine Reason.

God does not act by pure will, but his will is subordinate
to his reason.   To claim that God is above reason and has no
other rule than his pure will is to upset everything.[56]   This
false principle spreads darkness so thick that it confounds good
and evil, true and false, and makes of all things a chaos.[56]   According to this principle, the universe is perfect because God
willed it.[56]   Monsters, according to this view, are as true achieve-
ments as any other of the designs of God.[56]   There is in truth
in God an eternal order in which we behold beauty, truth, and
justice and we do not fear to criticise his work and to point out
its defects.[57]   This eternal order is the law of God himself,
written in his substance in divine characters.[57]
It is interesting to note some of the contrasts and affinities
involved in this doctrine of Malebranche.   Descartes, it will be
remembered, proclaimed an ultimate voluntarism in theology.
He declares that the divine will is absolutely independent of,
and prior to, the divine understanding.   "Thus," he says, "to
illustrate, God did not create the world in time because he saw
that it would be better thus than if he created it from all eter-

---

[52] *Entretiens*, p. 224.
[54] *Entretiens*, p. 225.
[55] *Entretiens*, p. 226.   Cf. Bouillier, pp. 119 and 125.   On the theory of Providence in general see Ollé-Laprune, *op. cit.*, Vol. I, p. 381ff.
[56] *Entretiens*, p. 231.
[57] *Entretiens*, p. 232.

nity; nor did he will the three angles of a triangle to be equal
because he knew that they could not be otherwise. On the contrary, because he created the world in time, it is for that reason
better than if he had created it from all eternity, and it is because he willed the three angles of a triangle to be necessarily
equal to two right angles that this is true and cannot be otherwise; and so in other cases . . . "[58] Malebranche would have
agreed with the contrary view expressed by the English Platon-
ist, Cudworth   Cudworth says, in his beautiful language "Now
it is certain that if the Natures and Essences of all things, as to
their being such and such, do depend upon a Will of God that
is essentially Arbitrary, there can be no such thing as Science
or Demonstration, nor the Truth of any Mathematical or Metaphysical Proposition be known any otherwise, than by some
Revelation of the Will of God concerning it, and by a certain
Enthusiastick or Fanatick Faith and Perswasion thereupon, that
God would have such a thing to be true or false at such a time,
or for so long. And so nothing would be true or false Naturally
but Positively only, all Truth and Science being meer Arbitrari-
ous things. . . . Wherefore, as for that argument that unless
the Essences and Verities of things depend upon the arbitrary
Will of God, there would be something that was not God, independent upon God; if it be well considered, it will prove a meer
Bugbear, and nothing so terrible and formidable as Cartesius
seemed to think it. For there is no other genuine Consequence
deducible from this Assertion, that the Essences and Verities
are independent upon the Will of God, but that there is an eternal and immutable Wisdom in the Mind of God. . . . Now all
the Knowledge and Wisdom that is in Creatures, whether Angels
or Men, is nothing else but a Participation of the one Eternal,
Immutable, and Increated Wisdom of God, or several signatures
of that one Archetypal Seal, or like so many Reflections of one
and the same Face, made in several glasses, whereof some are
clearer, some obscurer, some standing nearer, some further off "[59]

We have now before us Malebranche's metaphysics and
theology in their main outlines. The remaining dialogues are
either expansions of ideas we have already discussed or else belong in the special history of theology rather than in the general history of philosophy   The *Dixième Entretien* discusses
the magnificence of God in the grandeur and indefinitely large
number of his works, the simplicity and fecundity of the ways
by which he conserves and develops them, the divine providence
in the first impression of movement on matter, and the idea that
this first step which was not determined by general laws was

[58] *Op cit.*, Vol II, p 248
[59] *Treatise concerning Eternal and Immutable Morality*, written before 1688, published 1731   *Cf* Selby-Biggs, *British Moralist* Vol II, p 256f   For an account of
Cudworth see Tulloch, *Rational Theology in England in the XVIIth Century*, Vol II,
pp 193-301.

yet guided by infinite wisdom.[59]   The *Onzième Entretien* continues the same subject and discusses Providence as revealed in the arrangement of bodies and in the infinite combinations of physical and moral, and of the natural and the supernatural.[60] The *Douzième Entretien* discusses divine Providence as revealed in the laws of mind and body, and the manner in which God distributes temporal goods through the angels and spiritual grace through Jesus Christ.[61]   The *Treizième Entretien* shows among other things the Providence of God as revealed in the infallibility of his Church.[62]   And lastly the *Quatorzième Entretien* shows how the incomprehensibility of the mysteries is a demonstrative proof of their truth, and discusses the Incarnation of Jesus Christ, defends his divinity against the Socinians, and shows that no creature, not even the Angels themselves, can adore God save through Jesus Christ.[63]

---

[59] *Entretiens*, p. 233ff.
[60] *Entretiens*, p. 296ff.
[62] *Entretiens*, p. 333ff.
[63] *Entretiens*, p. 265ff.

Chapter VIII Malebranche's System of Ethics.

We have now to examine Malebranche's system of moral philosophy.[1] This we find expressed in the *Traité de Morale* of 1684 This work is among the earliest attempts in modern philosophy to found the moral life upon a rational basis and deserves very careful consideration as a document in the history of rationalism. In fact, Malebranche's ethics completes the system of Descartes, although of course it also transforms it. Descartes, it will be remembered, had relegated the practical life of the individual to the Church and the State. He did not feel obliged to discuss practical matters, "for," he said, "as regards that which concerns conduct, every one is so confident of his own good sense that there might be found as many reformers as heads, if it were permitted that others than those whom God has established as the sovereigns of his people, or at least to whom he has given sufficient grace and zeal to be prophets, should be allowed to make any changes in that."[2]

Nevertheless there was contained in Cartesianism the impetus to a rational foundation of the moral life as well as of the theoretical life, and this tendency is expressed in the ethical system of Malebranche.

Love of the Eternal Order.

The *Traité de Morale* opens with a reaffirmation of the doctrine of Vision in God. The Reason which enlightens all men is the Word, the divine *Logos,* or the wisdom of God[3] This reason or light I have in common with all men; the pain I feel, for example, is a modification of my own substance but the truth that I contemplate is a good common to all minds.[4] Thus by means of reason I enter into communion with God and all intelligences and this spiritual society consists in participation in the intelligible substance of the Word, in which all spirits can nourish themselves.[4] Now in thus contemplating the divine substance I can discover a part of what God thinks, and also a part of what he wills, for he wills according to the Order[4] That is, he loves things in proportion as they are lovable, and I can discover what things are more perfect, more estimable, and more lovable than others.[4]

---

[1] In general, on Malebranche's ethics, *cf* Novaro, *op cit*, and Ollé-Laprune, *op. cit*, Vol II, p 468ff

[2] *Discourse on Method*, Part VI, p 119 of the Haldane and Ross translation, Vol I.

[3] *Morale*, p 1

[4] *Morale*, p 2.

Now the intelligible substance of the Word contains within itself two sorts of truths or relations, relations of magnitude and relations of perfection. These relations of perfection constitute the immutable Order which God consults when he acts; the immutable Order which should be the rule of the loves and actions of all intelligences.[5] There is thus a true and a false, a just and an unjust, with regard to all intelligences, for all intelligences necessarily behold the same relations of magnitude, or speculative truths, and the same relations of perfection or practical truths.[5] As examples of relations of magnitude, or of speculative truths, Malebranche gives us the simple arithmetical equality and inequality between two plus two and four and five.[6] Thus Truth and Order are real, immutable, and necessary relations contained in the substance of the divine Word, and he who beholds these relations beholds what God beholds and he who regulates his love by them loves what God loves.[6]

Man is free.[7] He can seek truth in spite of his love of repose; he can love the eternal Order despite concupiscence.[7] He is thus a subject of merit and demerit, and, since God loves his creatures in proportion as they are lovable, and wills that all who resemble him be rewarded and all who are culpable, punished,[7] he who labors to perfect himself, to make himself like God, works at his own happiness.[7] For since God loves beings in proportion as they are lovable, and the more perfect are the more lovable, the more perfect will be the more powerful, the more fortunate, and the more contented.[8] He then who ceaselessly consults reason, who loves the Order, participating as he does in the divine perfection, will participate in the divine happiness and glory.[8]

Man is capable of three things, of knowledge, of love, and of feeling; he can know the good, love the good, and enjoy the good.[8] To a certain extent it depends upon the individual in regard to the first two, but it depends entirely upon God whether he shall enjoy the good.[8] But since God is just, he who knows and loves him shall enjoy him.[8] It is strange that although man well knows that pleasure and pain do not depend upon him, but that to a certain extent it does depend upon him as to whether or not he shall know the truth and love the eternal Order, he yet seeks only pleasure and neglects the principle of eternal happiness.[8]

Here we come upon the ultimate principle of duty, for the sake of which we have been created. It is love of the eternal Order. This is *"la vertu mère, la vertu universelle, la vertu universelle, la vertu fondamental."*[9] It is knowledge and love

[5] *Morale*, p. 4.
[6] *Morale*, p. 6.
[7] *Morale*, p. 7.
[8] *Morale*, p. 8.
[9] *Morale*, p. 9.

of relations of perfection, or practical truth, that constitutes our perfection.[9] But if virtue is obedience to a divine law, obedience to nature is merely obedience to divine decrees and is necessity rather than virtue.[9] We can resist the action of God without disobeying the eternal Order, for, although God wills only according to the eternal Order, he often acts contrary to it.[9] For the eternal Order itself dictates that God act in a uniform and constant manner.[9] Thus, in consequence of his eternal laws, he may act in particular cases in opposition to the eternal Order. Hence to maintain that we should follow nature is to maintain that we should follow what is necessarily contrary to Order in many instances.[10] If God moved bodies by particular volitions, it would be a crime to escape by flight from a falling wall, for God has assuredly the right to take back the life he has given.[10] On the same theory it would be an insult to the divine intelligence to correct the course of rivers But since God acts in accordance with general rules we can resist his action without resisting his will.[11] We can, to some extent, know the eternal Order, but the divine decrees are absolutely unknown to us; hence we must abandon the chimerical virtue of following nature, and follow rather reason.[11]

The love of the eternal Order is not only the principal moral virtue, it is, in fact, the only true virtue.[12] If a man gives his goods to the poor either because of vanity or natural compassion he is not liberal, for it is not eternal Order that rules him, but merely pride or disposition—of the machine.[12] Officers, who voluntarily expose themselves to danger, are not courageous if ambition animates them, nor are soldiers if it is abundance of spirits and fermentation of the blood that animates them.[12] This boasted noble ardor is either vanity or play of the machine (*jeu de machine*). a little more wine is often all that is needed to produce more of it.[12] He who endures the outrages which are done to him is often neither moderate nor patient[12] It may be his laziness which renders him unmoved, and his ridiculous and stoical pride which consoles him and places him in idea above his enemies; this again is only the disposition of the machine, condition of his spirits, coldness of the blood, or melancholy[13] It is the same with all the virtues. If love of Order is not the principle of them, they are false and vain, in all ways unworthy of a rational being, who bears the image of God himself, and communes with him by reason.[13] Uninspired by love of Order, they draw their origin from the disposition of the body.[13] The Holy Spirit does not form them; and whoever makes of them the object of his desires and the

[10] *Morale*, p 10
[11] *Morale*, p 11
[12] *Morale*, p 14
[13] *Morale*, p 15

subject of his glory has a base soul, a mean spirit, and a corrupt heart.[13]

Malebranche draws a distinction between virtue and the duties. To confuse these two is indeed one of the greatest mistakes of all those moralists who have not applied the method of clear ideas.[14] Virtue is the inner love of the eternal Order; the duties are merely the special outer actions which can be performed with or without love of the Order.[14] Virtue necessarily makes him virtuous who possesses it, but it is possible to perform actions of humility, generosity, and liberality without possessing virtue.[14] Men imagine that they are following virtue when they are in reality only following their natural inclinations, which lead them to perform certain duties.[14] Most men are deceived by confused ideas as to what virtue is and consider themselves better than others who are in reality more virtuous, for it is impossible to follow the dictates of eternal Order for any length of time without *appearing* to fail in some essential "duty."[14] For to appear prudent, honest and charitable before men, it is necessary sometimes to praise vice, and nearly always to be silent when it is praised.[14] To be esteemed liberal, we must be prodigal; without being foolhardy we shall hardly pass as valiant men; and if we are not superstitious, we shall be regarded as libertines.[14]

Now universal reason is always the same, and eternal Order is immutable; but morality (*morale*) changes according to time and place.[15] Among the Germans, virtue consists in knowing how to drink.[15] Among the nobility, generosity consists solely in shedding the blood of those who have insulted us.[15] Each person has his private morality, his private devotion, and his private virtue.[16] Whence comes this diversity? It is because men do not always consult reason, because we permit ourselves to be guided by the imagination.[16] We are too prone to believe that eternal law is beyond our reach, and we believe, like the gross and carnal Jews, that it is as difficult to discover the eternal law as to mount into heaven or descend into hell.[16] It is true that eternal Order is not of easy access, it dwells within, but we are always turned outwards.[16] We must silence sense, imagination, and passion, and not imagine that we can be reasonable without consulting Reason.[16]

Some hold that reason is corrupt and should be subjected to faith, that philosophy is only a servant, that we must deny our light.[17] Perpetual equivocation, says Malebranche. Man is not his own light and his own reason, and religion is itself the true philosophy.[17] Reason is infallible, immutable, and incor-

[14] *Morale*, p 17
[15] *Morale*, p 18
[16] *Morale*, p 19
[17] *Morale*, p 20

ruptible, and should always be supreme.[17] God himself follows reason.[17] We must not close our eyes to the light but accustom ourselves to distinguish true light from the false gleams of confused feeling, or of sense.[17] Intelligence is preferable to faith [17] Faith passes but understanding abides forever. Faith is indeed a great good because it leads to understanding, and because without it we cannot be worthy of understanding certain essential truths without which we can neither acquire solid virtue nor eternal felicity [17] Nevertheless, if we leave the mysteries out of account, faith totally without light, if it is possible, cannot render us solidly virtuous [18] Those who have not enough light to conduct themselves, can acquire virtue just as well as those who are better able to enter into themselves and contemplate the beauty of the eternal Order, but, all other things equal, he who enters most into himself is most solidly virtuous, and of two loves for the eternal Order that is more meritorious into which more intelligence enters.[18]

Love of the eternal Order, Malebranche holds, is identical with the Christian virtue of charity, which, however, is described in the Scriptures in somewhat vague language.[19] This immutable Order consists in relations of perfection holding between the intelligible ideas contained in the substance of the Word.[20] Now there are two distinct sorts of love which are due to perfection.[21] There is the love of good-will (*bienviellance*) and the love of union.[21] In the love of union we regard the object of our passion as the cause of our happiness and we desire to be united with it that the object may exert its full influence.[21] But the love of good-will is for people according to their merit, and we feel this love for them even when they cannot benefit us.[21] Thus the power of effecting our happiness calls forth the love of union, while the other perfections call forth the love of good-will [21] Now since God is the sole efficient cause in the universe, since finite beings derive their whole efficacy from him, he alone is the proper object of love of union. To love a finite object with a love of union is only possible on the false doctrine that they can causally influence us.[21]

The reverse is true, however, of the love of good-will.[22] True, God is infinitely more deserving of the love of good-will than any finite creature can be.[22] But he really communicates to them some perfection [22] The eternal Order itself demands that we esteem and love creatures in proportion to the perfection that they possess, in so far as these perfections are known to us.[22] It is entirely impossible to love them precisely according to their perfection, for our knowledge of the relations of

[17] *Morale*, p 21
[18] *Morale*, p 24f
[20] *Morale*, p. 27
[21] *Morale*, p 28
[22] *Morale*, p 29

perfection is much less e x a c t than our knowledge of the
relations of magnitude, and we do not know completely what
perfection the individual possesses.[22] Nevertheless beings who
are made in the image of God, and who are united with him,
are of more value than any other creatures.[22] Again, a member of Jesus Christ is more worthy of love than a thousand
impious persons.[22]

Self-love can be accommodated to the love of union, which
responds to and honors a power capable of affecting us, if self-
love is enlightened.[23] Man has a necessary desire for happiness
and he sees clearly that God alone can render him happy; he
can therefore desire to be united with God.[23] Even if a man
does not know that God rewards merit and only thinks of the
power and goodness of God, his faith can lead him, for the sake
of his own happiness, to unite himself with God[24] Thus self-
love is not directly opposed to the love of union The reverse is
true of the love of good-will.[24] The eternal Order of justice
dictates that recompense be proportional to merit, happiness to
virtue; but self-love does not willingly endure limits to its happiness and glory.[24] However enlightened this love may be, if
it is not just, it is necessarily contrary to Order, and it cannot
be just without diminishing or destroying itself.[24]

The love of Order is not like particular dispositions that
can be lost or acquired; for Order is not a particular creature
that one can wholly begin or cease to love.[24] It is in God and is
ceaselessly impressed upon us.[25] We cannot completely renounce
reason nor wholly cease to love Order.[25] In fact, the love of
Order naturally rules us save when self-love or concupiscence
resist.[25] Thus the beauty of justice often affects the unjust
themselves, so that self-love itself finds it to its own advantage
to conform to Order.[25] All light comes from the Word; all
movement from the Holy Spirit; hence, in so far as a man thinks
he is united to reason, in so far as he loves, he loves, to some
extent, the eternal Order.[25] For we cannot fall into error without using reason nor love the evil save by our love of the good.[25]
Thus self-love cannot destroy love of Order.[26]

It is not enough to love the Order with a natural love which
easily accommodates itself to self-love.[26] Our love must be free,
enlightened and reasonable.[26] Our love of the eternal Order
must be *dominant*; for however wicked a man may be, he will
feel some passing inclination for the Order.[26] The demons themselves have still some love of the Order.[26] God judges the disposition of the soul, not its actual transitory actions. A single
act does not form a habit and a man is only just before God

[22] *Morale*, p. 30
[24] *Morale*, p. 31
[25] *Morale*, p 32
[26] *Morale*, p 33

when he has a permanent disposition to love the good in preference to the evil.[27] Furthermore, love may be either natural or free.[27] Natural love is a natural product of pleasure.[27] Free love expresses a choice, it depends on reason, or liberty, on the power of the soul to resist pressure.[27] The essential differentia of this species of love is the consent of the will.[27] Now God only regards free love in the cases where both free and natural love are present.[28] From all these considerations, Malebranche concludes that the sole love which justifies us before God is an habitual, free and dominant love of the immutable Order.[28]

The Fourth Chapter of the First Part of the *Traité de Morale* is an illuminating discussion of the relation of action and habit. In the first place, we must recognize that actions produce habits, and secondly that habits express themselves in actions.[29] Nevertheless the soul does not always act in accordance with its dominant habit. The sinner could always have refrained from any particular sin, and the righteous man was always capable of an unjust action, for the sinner was never wholly without love of Order, nor was the righteous man wholly without self-love.[30] But, as Malebranche adds, in accordance with his Jansenistic tendency, free-will alone cannot save a man. No philosopher, however enlightened he may have been, whether Socrates, or Plato, or Epictetus, nor even those whom we may suppose to have shed their blood for the sake of the eternal Order, shall be saved without the grace that faith alone bestows.[31]

If love of Order is the supreme virtue, then the means of acquiring it are of the first importance. Of these Malebranche distinguishes three Force of Mind, Liberty of Mind, and Obedience to Order The first two are concerned with the discovery of ethical truth; the last is concerned with making ethical truth the dominant and habitual principle of our practical lives The first two principles, especially, sow the imprint of Descartes' methodological canons. Let us examine them in order.

Force of Mind

To explain this cardinal virtue, Malebranche returns to the basic principles of the whole system. Faith and reason alike assure us, he says, that God is the unique cause of all things, while experience shows that he acts according to certain laws. Thus the collision of two bodies is the occasional cause which necessarily determines the efficacy of the general laws according to which God produces thousands of effects in his works.[32] Thus it is God alone who enlightens spirits; nevertheless, we may seek

[27] *Morale*, p 35
[28] *Morale*, p 36
[29] *Morale*, pp 38 and 39
[30] *Morale*, p 40
[31] *Morale*, p 43
[32] *Morale*, p 47

in ourselves the occasional cause which determines him to communicate understanding to us.[32] He has attached the presence of ideas to the attention of the mind, and in proportion to our attention we shall have light.[33] So true is this that man, in his ingratitude and stupidity, imagines that he is the cause of his knowledge [33] God has made us occasional causes of our knowledge for many reasons, of which the first is that without being occasional causes of our knowledge, we could not be masters of our wills, for had we no power of thinking, we should have none of willing and should not be in a position to merit the true goods for which we were made.[33]

The attention of the mind is, then, a natural prayer for enlightenment.[33] Now those who are made for this severe toil, or labor of attention and who are always attentive to the truth which ought to guide them may be said to possess Force of Mind (force d'esprit).[34] To acquire this force of mind we must begin at an early age. To begin is itself difficult. We become discouraged and declare ourselves unfit for meditation. But if we do this we are renouncing virtue, at least in part [34] For without the work of attention, we shall never comprehend the grandeur of religion, the littleness of all that is not God, the absurdity of the passions, and of all our internal miseries. Without this labor, the soul will live blindly and in a disorderly fashion [34] There is no other way to obtain the light that should conduct us, we shall be eternally under disquietude and in strange embarrassment; for we fear everything when we walk in darkness and surrounded by precipices It is true that faith guides and supports, but it does so only as it produces some light by the attention it excites in us; for light alone is what can assure minds like ours, which have so many enemies to fear.[34]

How can we acquire Force of Mind? We must avoid all that divides the capacity of the mind, that is, all the objects, that flatter the senses and awaken the passions.[35] We must avoid as much as possible all the sciences and employments which are merely showy, in which memory alone works, and where the imagination is too active [36] Nothing is more opposed to reason than imagination too well instructed, too delicate, too active, or rather, too malign and corrupt.[36] A man must toil in the spirit to gain the life of the spirit, but to use one's mind to gain honor or gold is servile [36] That a workman should work with his body to gain the life of the body is according to Order, but that a magistrate, or a man of affairs, or a merchant spend the energy of their minds in the acquisition of goods which are harmful to their souls is a striking piece of madness.[37]

[33] *Morale*, p 48
[34] *Morale*, p 49.
[35] *Morale*, p 50
[36] *Morale*, p 51
[37] *Morale*, p 52

The one rule upon which Malebranche insists is that we meditate only on clear ideas and incontestable facts [37] To meditate on confused sentiments and on doubtful facts is a futile work. it is to contemplate phantoms.[38] The immutable and necessary Order should be the subject of our meditations, but there is nothing more abstract and less sensuous than this Order.[38] It is true that the Order became sensible and visible in the actions and precepts of Jesus Christ; the Word made flesh, however, is only an indispensable model according to which by "la folie apparente de la foi" we are lead to reason.[38] Jesus Christ accommodated Himself to our weakness to draw us from it.[38] Faith speaks to the mind through the body in order that man may free himself from the body and enter the intelligible world [38]

Knowledge of the eternal Order, which is our indispensable law, is a mixture of clear ideas and feelings.[39] All men know that it is better to be just than to be rich; but not all men know this by clear ideas. Children and ignorant people know when they do wrong, but it is rather the secret reproach of reason than clear understanding that warns them.[39] For Order may be speculatively apprehended and in this way it enlightens the mind without stirring it to action, and in so far as it is thus apprehended, the eternal order is clear.[39] But Order can also be apprehended as the natural and necessary principle and rule of the *actions* of the soul, as such it moves the soul without enlightening it. Thus we can know the eternal Order either by clear idea or confused feeling.[39] This confused feeling of the Order, however, is peculiarly open to the deceiving influence of passion and concupiscence.[39] Thus we must seek for clear ideas · we must exercise the virtue of Force of Mind.

Liberty of Mind.

The second of Malebranche's cardinal virtues, which is also drawn from the Cartesian methodology, is what he calls Liberty of Mind. However much Force of Mind we may possess, we cannot work without cessation, and there are subjects so obscure that we cannot penetrate into them; we must have another virtue, *Liberté d'esprit*, according to which we withhold our judgment until we are forced to give it.[40] When we examine a very complex question, and the mind finds itself surrounded by difficulties on all sides, reason permits that we abandon the question, but also dictates that we suspend our judgment.[40] To make as great a use of Liberty as possible is thus an indispensable precept of logic and morality.[41] We must never believe until the evidence forces us to believe.[41]

[38] *Morale*, p 58.
[39] *Morale*, p 56
[40] *Morale*, p 59
[41] *Morale*, p 60

This holds of man as reasonable, of man in so far as he conducts himself according to reason.[41] For the citizen, the soldier, the man of religion has, as such, other principles and it is reasonable that he follow them even though he does not yet see clearly that they are conformable to reason.[41] But where faith has made no decision, and custom prescribes nothing we must adhere only to what we clearly and evidently see.[41] And if we clearly and evidently see that human authority and custom are mistaken, we must renounce everything rather than reason.[41] Of course, the infallible authority of the Church *cannot* contradict reason [41]

Force of Mind is to the search for truth what Liberty of Mind is to the possession of truth, or at least to exemption from error. For by the exercise that we make of Force of Mind we discover truth, and by the exercise of Liberty of Mind, we are exempt from error.[41] Liberty of Mind is necessary because the mind lacks Force; it is necessary that the mind may suspend its judgment where it lacks the power to know the truth.[41] The finite mind can never deliver itself from ignorance but by the exercise of Liberty it can escape error.[42]

These two cardinal virtues, Force and Liberty of Mind, are not common faculties among men; on the contrary, nothing is more rare, and no one possesses them in perfection.[42] Man is naturally capable of some mental exertion, but he cannot be considered, ordinarily, to be of a strong mind.[42] These virtues can only be acquired by practice, and their acquisition is a return of the soul to its primary state before the original sin.[43] To acquire them is not to change or destroy one's nature but to repair it.[43] Furthermore, these virtues are present to different individuals to different extents and in the same individual at different times to different extents.[43] If they are not increased in extent by exercise they necessarily diminish, for there are no virtues more contrary to concupiscence.[43] We can scarcely meditate without pain and suspension of judgment is still more difficult.[43] There are very few who undertake the search for truth, and few of these have the energy and courage to attain it it.[43] Weary and rebutted, the majority of those who undertook the quest try to console themselves with what they have attained.[43] They console themselves, perhaps, with a ridiculous scorn of truth, or with a base despair, or they become deceivers, having been deceived themselves.[44]

To acquire Liberty of Mind we must ceaselessly reflect on the prejudices of men and on the causes of these prejudices [44]. We believe that we understand things when we cease to marvel at them, that is, when we have become familiar with them.[44]

[41] *Morale*, p 61
[43] *Morale*, p 62
[44] *Morale*, p 63

It is pleasant to judge of everything; and we can not investigate without at least some pain.[44] Hence all ordinary language is *un galimatias perpétuel*, a stream of nonsense.[44] Everyone believes that he understands what he says or what he hears, and only rejects new terms which may, nevertheless, be more clear and intelligible than the old.[44] From the failure on the part of mankind to exert Liberty, Malebranche derives all those false explanations in which the scholastic philosophy abounded, such as, humidity and heat as the principles of generation and corruption of all things, and the *séminales* and *vertus prolifiques* which explain how species run true to type.[45] And, lastly, the belief in Nature as an explanatory term comes from the same origin.[46]

However important in science it may be for a man to suspend his judgment, it is much more important to suspend properly one's judgment in matters of morality.[46] The reason is that in these matters exact knowledge is difficult because our ideas are obscured by our passions.[47] We are often obliged to act before we clearly know what we should do; but, although we must, in such cases, act, we must not believe more than the evidence compels us to believe.[47] This must not be understood to mean that we are to remain in perpetual doubt, for between doubt and belief there is an infinite series of unnamed states.[47] As there is an infinite series of probabilities, the mind must put each state of affairs in its proper place; for although a given principle may not be evident, it may be evident that the principle is probable.[47] We must not imagine that the suspension of judgment involved in Liberty of Mind is easy "Let a man pass but one year," exclaims Malebranche, "in the commerce of the world, hearing all that is said and believing nothing; entering into himself at all times to find whether the inner truth uses the same language and always suspending his consent until light appears! I hold him much wiser than Aristotle, wiser than Socrates, more enlightened than the divine Plato "[47]

Obedience to Order

The third great fundamental virtue, according to Malebranche, is Obedience to Order. Facility in rendering oneself attentive, and in suspending judgment, although necessary for all solid virtue, is not the whole of virtue.[48] There is necessary an exact obedience to divine law, a stable and dominant disposition to regulate all the movements of the heart and all the steps of conduct according to the eternal Order.[48] For what would it benefit a man to have enough Force and Liberty of

[45] *Morale*, p 64
[46] *Morale*, p 65
[47] *Morale*, p 66
[48] *Morale* p 70

Mind to discover the most concealed truths and avoid even the
slightest errors if he did not live according to his lights and
withdrew himself from the obedience which he owes to the divine law"[48]

How can we acquire this dominant disposition? As we have
seen, habits are built out of acts.[49] We must often make firm
and constant resolutions to obey the Order, these repeated resolutions will gradually give us the disposition we are seeking[49]
This is easy to conceive, but hard to do; in fact, it cannot be
achieved without the aid of divine grace.[49] A man without divine grace and consequently without faith can very well desire
death or nothingness, rather than life, in the absence of what he
loves. We can desire not to exist, but we cannot desire to exist
in a miserable condition; for we have an irresistible desire to be
happy.[49] Now without faith that we shall find a greater happiness than that which we renounce, we shall never be able to renounce our dominant passion.[49] And faith is the effect of divine grace   Nevertheless, as Malebranche shows in some detail,
the exercise of Force and Liberty of Mind can prepare the mind
for faith, by teaching us to despise the passions and by means
of the purity which it introduces into our imaginations[50]

These three virtues, Force and Liberty of Mind, and Obedience to Order are so many phases of the original love of the
Order of Perfection which stands at the center of Malebranche's
ethical system. To know the truth and to serve it, such, for
Malebranche, constituted the essence of human merit. It is interesting to compare this system of ethics with a system which
Malebranche would certainly have regarded as the diametrical
opposite of his system, that of Spinoza   Both laid an equal
stress upon clear ideas as the foundation of the moral life. For
Spinoza, in so far as our mind has adequate ideas it is active;
in so far as it has inadequate ideas it is passive[51] In fact, in
clear ideas, Spinoza places not only the activity of the mind,
but also human freedom as distinct from human bondage, as well
as immortality and love of God. In so far as we know we are
free and active. In so far as we are free and active, we are
eternal, that is, we know and love God with his own eternal
knowledge and love of himself.[52] "The intellectual love of the
mind towards God is that very love of himself, not in so far as
he is infinite, but in so far as he can be explained through the
essence of the human mind regarded under the form of eternity;
in other words, the intellectual love of the mind towards God
is part of the infinite love wherewith God loves himself."[53]

The stress, however, which both of these great seventeenth

[48] *Morale*, p 71
[50] *Morale*, pp 72-79
[51] *Ethics*, Part III, Prop I
[52] *Ethics*, Part III, Defs I and II, and Part V, Prop XXXVI
[53] Part V, Prop XXXVI, trans Elwes

century rationalists placed upon the function of clear ideas in the moral and religious life should not blind us to the essential diversity of their systems. For Malebranche the ultimate source of good lay in an absolute system of values in the divine mind which possessed an absolute authority over the individual. Spinoza, as is well known, rejected the teleological view of the world,[54] and defined the "good" as that which we certainly know to be useful to us, "evil" as that which we know to be a hindrance to us.[55] Spinoza thus regarded good and evil as not inhering in the world itself, but as based upon human desires. For Malebranche, on the other hand, there was, as we have seen, an immutable system of rationally apprehended values which did not in any way depend upon the choice of the individual. Malebranche is the faithful disciple of Plato and Augustine, while Spinoza's view shows the stamp of modern naturalism.

In the doctrine of love of the eternal Order we have the essential point of Malebranche's ethics The remainder of the *Traité de Morale* deals with either the religious and theological side of morality or with certain practical applications which Malebranche makes of his doctrine He thus discusses the means that religion furnishes to the acquisition of the love of Order.[56] Jesus Christ is the occasional cause of grace.[57] When we approach the Sacraments our actual love of Order becomes habitual in consequence of the permanent desires of Jesus Christ.[58] The fear of hell is as good a motive as the desire for eternal felicity, but in both cases we must distinguish the *motive* from the *end*.[59] Chapter IX shows why we must pray to the Virgin, the Angels and the Saints, although not as occasional causes of grace [60]

The Second Part of the *Traité de Morale* is concerned with *devoirs*, that is to say, with particular external actions. We have obligations to each of the divine attributes, to the divine power,[61] to the divine wisdom,[62] and to the divine love.[63] In the Sixth Chapter of Part II Malebranche takes up the problem of our duties to the two societies of which we are members, the "society of commerce," animated by passion, consisting of a community of particular and transitory goods, with the comfort and conservation of the life of the body as its end, and the "society of religion" sustained by faith, consisting in a com-

[54] Cf *Ethics*, Part I, Appendix.
[55] *Op cit*, Defs I and II, Part IV
[56] *Morale*, p. 81
[57] *Morale*, p 88
[58] *Morale*, p 81ff
[59] *Morale*, p 89f
[60] *Morale*, p 96f
[61] *Morale*, p 147ff
[62] *Morale*, p 159ff
[63] *Morale*, p 167ff

munity of true goods with eternal happiness as an end.[64] Everything should be related to the eternal spiritual society.[65] Our obligations to other men should be all taken as external, for it is very dangerous to make our service to men an inner concern.[66] Intercourse with the world is in general dangerous.[67] There are two sovereign powers, the Church and the State, which are ruled by the Prince and the Bishop, the Prince the image of Omnipotent God, the Bishop of Jesus Christ.[68] To these powers the individual owes an absolute allegiance. "As for the subjects," says Malebranche, "it seems to me that they should obey blindly, when only their interest is concerned."[69] Marriage is the symbol of the union of Jesus Christ and his Church and is a natural union evidently provided for by the Creator.[70] In the last chapter, Malebranche discusses the duties that each person owes to himself and which consist in working for one's own perfection and happiness [71]

[64] *Morale*, p 184ff
[65] *Morale*, p 185
[66] *Morale*, p 187
[67] *Morale*, p 189
[68] *Morale*, p. 211
[69] *Morale*, p 216
[70] *Morale*, p 219f
[71] *Morale*, p 262f. On Malebranche's ethics as a whole *cf* Ollé-Laprune, Vol I, p 447f